Basic Golf

Basic Golf

THOMAS D. FAHEY
California State University, Chico

MAYFIELD PUBLISHING COMPANY

Mountain View, California
London · Toronto

To my golfing buddies Joe Brady, George Brooks, and Bill
Colvin. If this book helps to improve your golf game, then my
time on earth will not have been wasted.

ISBN-13: 978-1-55934-107-3

ISBN-10: 1-55934-107-6

Copyright © 1995 by Mayfield Publishing Company

Library of Congress Cataloging-in-Publication Data
Fahey, Thomas D. (Thomas Davin)
    Basic golf / Thomas D. Fahey.
      p.   cm.
    Includes index.

    1. Golf.   I. Title
    GV965.F25 1995.
    796.352--dc20   94-19540
                                         CIP

Manufactured in the United States of America
10 9

Mayfield Publishing Company
1280 Villa Street
Mountain View, CA 94041

Sponsoring editor, Serina Beauparlant; production editor, Julianna
Scott Fein; manuscript editor, Carol Dondrea; text and cover designer,
Richard Kharibian & Associates; cover photograph, © David Madison,
1993; art editor, Robin Mouat; illustrators, Willa Bower and Cyndie
C. H. Wooley. The text was set in 10/12 Times New Roman by ColorType

Contents

Chapter **8**

Conditioning the Mind for Golf   **106**

Preface

For many people, golf is an obsession that brings joy, exhilaration, and a sense of achievement. The game provides an opportunity for golfers to test their skills in beautiful parklike settings, playing with friends, strangers, or by themselves. Playing golf can also reduce stress and contribute to physical fitness.

To beginners, of course, golf is a challenge. Beginning students ask lots of questions: What kind of equipment should I buy? How do I find instruction? What are the basic techniques of the game? How do I get in shape to play the game? What are the rules? This book answers these and other questions that every beginning golfer has.

Written specifically for the novice, *Basic Golf* presents the fundamentals of the game in a readable, succinct format. It is a useful primer on everything first-time players need to know about golf. The text's thorough but concise coverage provides students with the information they need to start playing right away. In the early chapters, students learn about the history of golf, instruction resources, and equipment needs. The core chapters cover the fundamentals of hitting and putting. Basic strategies are covered in detail, helped by clear instructions and numerous illustrations. The rules of golf and golf course etiquette are also covered, and a glossary of terms is provided at the end of the book.

In addition, two important topics are presented in *Basic Golf* that are not discussed in other beginning instruction texts: the importance of fitness and the game's mental aspects. The importance of fitness is often ignored by golf instructors, yet injuries and fatigue keep many players from realizing their full potential. Chapter 7, "Golf and Your Body," provides students with information on how golf can fit into a wellness lifestyle. The chapter includes practical advice about nutrition, conditioning, injuries, flexibility, and other fitness and health topics. Also included in this chapter are easy-to-do warm-up exercises.

The mental side of the game is also considered. Every golfer knows that golf is both a physical *and* mental game. Chapter 8, "Conditioning the Mind for Golf," discusses this important aspect. Information on confidence, imagery, and discipline—basic techniques of sports psychology—helps students learn how to prime themselves for success on the course. The chapter includes information from sports psychologists, champion golfers, and professional psychology journals.

A book always represents the work of many people besides the author. I am indebted to the editorial and production staff at Mayfield Publishing Company, including Erin Mulligan, Julianna Scott Fein, and Robin Mouat. I am grateful for the many valuable suggestions made by reviewers of the manuscript: Robert W. Christina, State University of New York–Buffalo; Joann Cox, New Mexico State University; Ron English, Ferris State University; Sylvia Ferdon, Baylor University; Allen Fox, Pepperdine University; R. Scott Kretchmar, Pennsylvania State University; Janet R. Nuzman, Washburn University; and Frank Pettigrew, Kent State University. I would like to thank my golfing buddies, including Joe Brady, George Brooks, Bill Colvin, Craig Buschner, and Don Chu. Watching them play has helped me appreciate the incredible flexibility of the human body. Finally, I would like to thank the professors and teachers who have given me a background in the study of sport and human movement: George Brooks, Frank Verducci, Larry Rarick, Franklin Henry, Carl Wallin, Robert Lualhati, and Larry Burleson.

The Joy of Golf: A Sport for a Lifetime

Golf is the passion of millions of people around the world. Golf exposes you to incredible beauty, serenity, excitement, and challenge—all at the same time. It is a sport you can play from childhood to old age. It provides exercise, the thrill of competition, and the chance to master difficult skills. Golf helps develop business relationships and friendships. Want to get into a conversation with a perfect stranger almost anywhere? Invite the person to talk about his or her golf game. This game will provide you with a physical and emotional outlet you can enjoy for the rest of your life.

Golf is an individual sport you can play almost anytime. If you have only a few hours, you can play a few holes at the local course or hit a bucket of balls at the **driving range.** If you can't sleep and it's the middle of the night, you can work on putting on the living room rug.

A game of golf is never the same from one time to the next. Each time you play you are exposed to new challenges. A golf **course** to a golfer is much like a mountain peak to a climber. The mountain is constant; it challenges the climber. In golf, the golf course presents the challenge. You hit the ball down a beautifully mowed, well-manicured fairway—and, sometimes, you hit from the rough or from a bunker or from the side of a hill. When you putt, you have the added challenge of reading the green correctly.

The challenge of the unexpected is part of the fun of golf. A ball landing in an unexpected place challenges you to overcome the misplaced shot—and you get immediate feedback. Over time, as your game improves, you are rewarded. At first, the reward may consist only of occasional great shots. Gradually, however, you will hit more good shots, and you will lower your score. Golf is an addictive sport.

This book discusses the fundamentals of this great sport. It covers topics that will give you a good introduction to the game—getting started, the mechanics of the golf swing, course management, rules and etiquette, controlling the body, and controlling the mind—and it introduces essentials such as getting instruction, buying equipment, playing on a course for the first time, and finding a place to practice. You will learn the mechanics of the swing, including how to grip the club; proper stance and swing; and how to adjust for irregular terrain. The book presents the intricacies of course strategy so you can compensate for less than perfect technique by playing the course intelligently. It introduces golf rules and etiquette so you learn to play by set standards that enhance the enjoyment of the game for everyone. You will learn how to integrate golf into a healthy lifestyle and how to prevent common golf injuries. Finally, you will be introduced to strategies for increasing concentration and focus while learning and playing golf.

Definitions of common terms used in golf can be found in the glossary at the back of the book. The basics of the game are discussed throughout the book.

BRIEF DESCRIPTION OF THE GAME

Golf is played with golf clubs and a golf ball. Golf clubs include woods, irons, and a putter. All clubs have a clubhead (the part of the club that makes contact with the ball), shaft, and grip. The clubheads of woods are typically made of wood or metal. Woods can usually hit the ball further than irons can. Irons are typically used for shots requiring accuracy. The putter is used for shots on or slightly off the green.

A standard game of golf is played on 18 holes. Each hole consists of a **teeing ground, fairway,** and **putting green** (Figure 1-1). A hole may also contain **hazards,** such as water hazards (ponds, streams, ocean, etc.) or **bunkers** (areas of bare ground usually covered with sand). At each hole, you put the **ball in play** by hitting a golf ball from a **tee box** (a place, usually grass, at the start of each hole designated for hitting your first shot) toward a hole using a

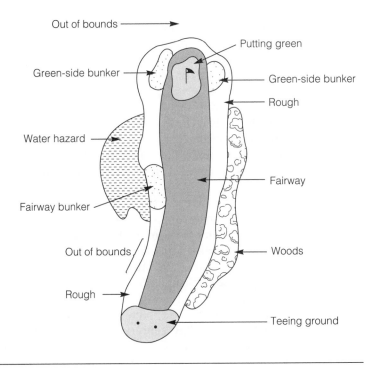

Out of bounds

Putting green

Green-side bunker

Green-side bunker

Rough

Water hazard

Fairway

Fairway bunker

Out of bounds

Woods

Rough

Teeing ground

Figure 1-1
A typical golf hole showing the tee, fairway, putting green, bunkers,
and water hazards.

golf club (either a wood or an iron). Once on the green, you putt
the ball into the hole (using a putter). The object of the game is to
hit the ball into the hole in as few strokes as possible.

After you have hit the ball from the tee, the general rule is to
play the ball where it lies. That's the basis of golf's excitement and
exasperation. You must play the ball from wherever it lies, including from the **rough** (unmowed and uncultivated areas), sand, or
behind a tree. In essence, the game today is not that much different from the way it began, when people would hit a rock with a
stick in a cow pasture toward a target.

HISTORY OF GOLF

Golf comes from the Dutch word "kolf." Games resembling golf
were played by the Romans, English, French, and Dutch. The

game as we know it today first appeared in Scotland or Holland. Evidently, golf was extremely popular by the 15th century because it inspired King James II of England to issue an edict condemning it: His subjects' obsession with the game was preventing them from practicing archery.

King James IV, during the early 16th century, popularized the game still further—he is the first player of record. His interest in the game probably had an effect on his subjects similar to President Eisenhower's on his fellow citizens in the United States in the 1950s. Eisenhower's frequent golf games attracted millions of people to the sport.

Mary, Queen of Scots, is the first woman golfer of record. She caused a scandal by playing golf only a few days after the murder of her husband. The daughter of King James IV, she grew up in St. Andrews and probably learned golf from her father.

The first known golf club, called the Company of Gentlemen Golfers, was established in Scotland in 1744. The famous Royal and Ancient Golf Club of St. Andrews was established in 1754. The club became the center of the golfing world, and its influence has extended well into the 20th century. The club has played a central role in the development of the rules of golf. Today, it and the **United States Golf Association (USGA)** are jointly responsible for writing and interpreting those rules.

In the United States, the early center for golf was the St. Andrews Golf Club in Yonkers, New York, which was started by John Reid, a Scot who is considered the father of golf in America. Other golf clubs established around the turn of the century included the Newport Golf Club, the Chicago Golf Club, and the Tuxedo Golf Club.

The United States Golf Association was established in 1894 for the purpose of making rules for the game and initiating amateur and open championships and competitions. Championships for men and women were first held in 1895. Except for the years during World Wars I and II, these championships have been held every year since.

There are over 13,000 golf courses in the United States, many set in some of the most beautiful locations in the world. Courses designed by people like Robert Trent Jones and Jack Nicklaus are marvels of civil engineering.

Many people play golf. During the early part of this century, the game was largely a rich person's sport. However, a series of American golfers—including Bobby Jones, Babe Didrikson-Zaharias, Ben Hogan, Mickey Wright, Arnold Palmer, Nancy Lopez, and Jack Nicklaus—captured the imagination of the public and made golf a game for the average person. U.S. presidents who have played golf, including Eisenhower, Kennedy, Ford, Bush, and Clinton, have further helped to popularize the sport.

Golf is also a spectator sport. Millions of people watch the professional golfers on television as they compete for large amounts of money in tournaments such as the U.S. Open, Masters, and British Open. During the past ten years, older professional players have formed a senior's tour, which is becoming almost as popular as that for younger players. Golf is also played competitively at the high school and college levels.

The Evolution of Equipment

Sports equipment technology has come a long way during the past 30 years. Today's equipment has made most sports easier to play and more accessible to the average person. In tennis, rackets have gone from primitive wooden pieces of equipment that warped easily, to oversized implements made of space-age material. Sports shoes are made with the anatomy and biomechanics of the foot in mind so that injury is prevented and performance enhanced.

Like tennis equipment, golf equipment has vastly improved since the early days of the game. Grips fit more easily in the hand, and shafts allow you to hit the ball more squarely and consistently. New materials in clubheads help you hit the ball straight, even when you don't hit it from the proper place on the club face. Numerous other equipment changes in golf have made the game more enjoyable. Shoes are better designed for improved performance and comfort; clothing fits better and is made of material more appropriate for exercise; golf bags are lighter and easier to carry. Golf balls are designed to travel better in the air, giving longer distance and greater accuracy.

In addition, biomechanics experts—people who study human movement—have developed computer programs that analyze your swing in detail and suggest improvements. Although these techniques have been available for many years in science laboratories, in a short time they will be readily available to the average person. Like other innovations, this will add to the game's enjoyment and bring more people into the sport.

Development of the Golf Ball   Early golf balls were made of wood. As might be expected, these broke easily, and it was difficult to become consistent using them. In the early 1600s, the feather ball was introduced. This consisted of boiled feathers stuffed into a leather cover. Although the ball was a great improvement over wooden balls, it was expensive and became easily saturated with water. In the mid-1800s, a ball made of gutta-percha, a latexlike material obtained from South American trees, was developed. This ball was inexpensive and improved consistency of play, thus bringing new players to the game. The rubber ball was introduced by the B. F. Goodrich company around the beginning of the 20th century. The ball consisted of rubber thread wound around a rubber core and was covered by a hard plastic. As materials and manufacturing techniques have become more sophisticated, balls have been produced that are more resilient and play even more consistently.

Development of Golf Clubs   Golf clubs were originally made completely of wood. With the advent of the gutta-percha ball, however, iron heads became commonplace. These new clubs were more attractive, easier to maintain, and improved consistency. As the harder rubber ball became popular, the heads of the woods had to become stronger, and durable persimmon and maple heads were introduced. Today, lamination techniques have made them even stronger.

During much of the first 30 to 40 years of this century, club shafts were made of hickory. This was an improvement over earlier models, but the shafts tended to twist during the swing, which required a lot of skill to hit them well consistently. In addition, the clubs aged quickly because of the constant torque (twisting). A two-year-old club with a hickory shaft would not play the same as it did the day it was bought.

In 1929 steel shafts were approved, and these had a major effect on the game. Because the shaft was more rigid, it didn't twist as much during the swing, so players could play more consistently, and enjoy the game more. Today, shafts are made from a variety of materials, including steel, aluminum, fiberglass, titanium, and graphite.

Development of the Golf Course   The first golf courses were little more than cow pastures. Over time, these became more defined, but it was not until 1764 that the standard 18-hole course became generally accepted. Before this, the number of holes on a course varied. For example, the St. Andrews course in Scotland originally consisted of 11 holes laid in a straight line along the seashore. The golfer played 11 holes one way, then played the same holes in getting back to the clubhouse.

Early courses were restricted to the upper social classes. As more people were exposed to the game, it became popular with all strata of society. Today, private country clubs exist in most larger communities, but public golf courses and private courses open to the public are commonplace.

Shorter nine-hole courses have also been developed. These are particularly attractive to beginners. Some of these courses have a standard variety of par 3, 4, and 5 holes. **Par** is the score an expert golfer would be expected to make for a hole; it is based on the distance from the tee to the green. Other courses, called executive courses, have holes averaging 100 yards. Driving ranges also allow people to practice away from the golf course and are a great place for the beginner to learn to play golf.

Worksheet

1. On each hole, the first shot is made from the _____.

2. What is a primary rule in golf and a source of the game's challenge? _____
    _____

3. Golf, as we know it today, first appeared in _____ or _____.

4. The _____ and _____
    are jointly responsible for writing and interpreting the rules of golf.

5. Shorter nine-hole golf courses are sometimes called _____.

2

Getting Started

Golf is an exciting sport with a long tradition. To beginners, it may seem grand and strange and just a little confusing. On television, you see skilled golfers playing on lush, beautiful—even awesome—courses. Around the golf course or practice range, you hear golfers talk endlessly about the game, using strange terms. And as a beginner, you may be confused about what clubs to buy, where to take lessons, what clothes to wear, how to play a golf course for the first time, and where to practice.

Relax! Every golfer started with these same feelings. The important thing to keep in mind is that learning to play golf is fun, exciting, and challenging. Just take it one step at a time. In this chapter you will learn the basics of getting started in golf.

GETTING INSTRUCTION

Before you do anything else, take some lessons. Success in golf requires consistency, and the best way to develop this is by learning the fundamentals of the game from a good instructor. A solid foundation in the basics of golf will afford you years of challenge and enjoyment.

Private golf lessons are expensive—but luckily there are alternatives. A golf class, for example, is a good place for an introduction to the game. Golf classes are generally inexpensive. If you are in college, you may find that a golf class counts toward your physical education requirement. If you are a working adult, you can take a class at a local community college. Later, you may wish to supplement what you learned in the golf class with private lessons from a professional at a golf course or driving range.

The level of instruction in college golf classes is usually excellent. Your instructor may also be the college golf coach and have years of experience working with all levels of golfers. In the class, you will be taught the fundamentals of the game.

Another alternative to private lessons is to take group lessons at a golf course. Here, in six or seven lessons, the course professional teaches the basics to groups of three to five golfers.

Private lessons, of course, are the ideal way to learn to play golf. If possible, sign up for a series of such lessons so you can cover most of the fundamentals. Although private lessons are expensive, they may actually save you money in the long run because you will get excellent advice about equipment and technique.

Once you have begun playing golf, you can improve your game by attending a golf clinic. Clinics are often included in vacation packages to places like Hawaii, Florida, California, Europe, and Mexico. These packages provide several hours of instruction per day on different aspects of the game and include daily rounds of golf on beautiful courses. Closer to home, golf clinics may also sometimes be held at local courses.

No matter how you get your initial instruction, you can learn a lot by reading books and magazines about golfing fundamentals. You may also find helpful videotapes on golf techniques. Actually seeing how shots are made has obvious advantages.

After a few lessons, you can begin to think about equipment and playing golf for the first time. Work closely with your instructor to ensure that your purchases are appropriate for your body size and skill level.

EQUIPMENT AND SUPPLIES

The equipment you need to play golf includes golf clubs, bag, and balls. As you get more involved in the game, you might purchase golf shoes and a golf glove as well. Proper clothing will allow you to move freely and, in general, add to your comfort on the course. Other supplies you will need, such as a score card, pencil, tees, and a ball marker are available free of charge (or for a small fee) at the golf course.

Golf Clubs

The rules allow you to carry no more than 14 clubs. Professional golfers often carry the 1- to 9-irons, a pitching wedge, a sand wedge, the 1- and 3-woods, and a **putter.** When you buy a set of irons, you typically get the 3- to 9-irons and a pitching wedge, so even adding a putter and a couple of woods keeps you well within the 14-club limit. A bare bones beginner set usually includes the 3-, 5-, 7-, and 9-irons, the 1- and 3-woods, and a putter. Beginners have more success with a 5-wood than with a 1-wood (called a "driver") but, unfortunately, beginner sets aren't packaged that way. Adding a pitching wedge to the basic set is a good idea because it is a good all-around club for hitting from sand and from short distances around the green. Regardless of what clubs you choose, however, the most important thing to remember is to buy clubs that are appropriate for your size, strength, and swing.

Irons   **Irons** are used for accuracy. They are numbered 1 to 9 and are classified as long (1–3 irons), medium (4–6 irons), and short (7–9). The longer the iron, the longer the shaft length and steeper the angle of the club face (Figure 2-1). Long irons tend to

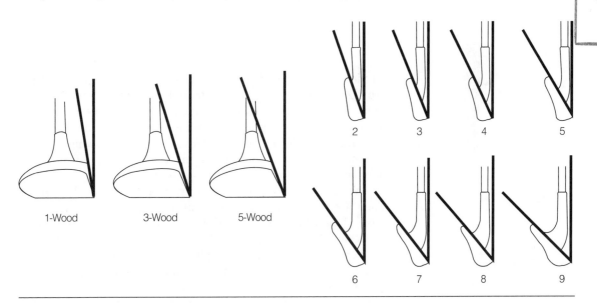

1-Wood   3-Wood   5-Wood

2   3   4   5

6   7   8   9

Figure 2-1

Club faces of various woods and irons. Lower numbered clubs have steeper club faces and longer shafts, which allows them to hit the ball further and lower to the ground. Shorter clubs (higher numbers) are used to hit the ball higher in the air.

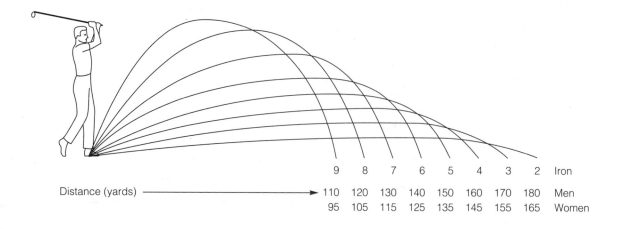

	9	8	7	6	5	4	3	2	Iron
Distance (yards) ⟶	110	120	130	140	150	160	170	180	Men
	95	105	115	125	135	145	155	165	Women

Figure 2-2

Distances the average golfer will hit the ball using various irons. Shorter irons cause the ball to go higher and travel shorter distances than longer irons. The distance you hit the ball with each iron may vary considerably from the values on this chart due to factors such as strength, body size, and skill.

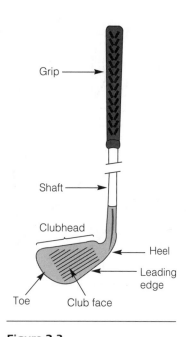

Grip ⟶

Shaft ⟶

Clubhead

Heel

Leading edge

Toe   Club face

Figure 2-3

An iron consists of a grip, shaft, and clubhead.

hit the ball further and at a lower trajectory than short irons (Figure 2-2). Longer irons also tend to make the ball roll further. Because shorter irons are used to hit the ball higher in the air, the ball doesn't roll as far. In general, beginners have a great deal of trouble hitting with the long irons because the arc of the swing is larger and more difficult to control. For this reason, most golf sets you purchase will not include a 1- or 2-iron.

Wedges are utility clubs that are usually classified as irons. They are important clubs when hitting within 100 yards of the hole. The **pitching wedge** is shorter, has a steeper club-face angle, and a slightly shorter shaft length than a 9-iron. A **sand wedge** has an even steeper angle than the pitching wedge and is designed to give loft to the ball when making bunker (sand) or pitch shots (shots made within 100 yards of the hole that travel mainly through the air). Sand wedges come in a variety of club-face angles. Some golf pros carry two different kinds of sand wedges so they can vary the height of the ball as it leaves the bunker.

An iron consists of a grip, shaft, and clubhead (Figure 2-3). Factors to be considered when buying clubs include grip, shaft and shaft flex, club weight, club lie, and type of clubhead back.

The Grip   As we discuss in Chapter 3, the grip is the foundation of a good golf swing. The grip is usually made of rubber with tiny bits of cork imbedded in it. The cork helps absorb sweat from your hands and gives you a better grip on the club. Some golfers like leather grips, which can be custom ordered from a pro shop. Although these grips require much more maintenance than the more standard rubber cork grips, proponents say they provide a "tackier" feeling—and thus better grip—than the others. Most golfers, however, should stick with rubber cork grips. Leather grips become easily saturated with water, dry and crack easily, and tend to unravel in a relatively short time.

Cord grips are relatively new. These are more expensive than rubber grips but may be worth the extra money. They provide a high degree of abrasiveness and are almost maintenance-free. A problem with these grips is that they may be too abrasive, particularly if you grip the club improperly and it slips in your hand during the swing. They also have to be replaced more often than rubber grips.

Grips come in different sizes, and it's important to get the size appropriate for your size hands. A grip that doesn't fit will twist in your hand during the swing and make it difficult for you to hit the ball with precision. A set of clubs bought off the shelf at a sporting goods store will have a standard grip size, which may not work for you. The best thing to do is let the people at a good pro shop help you determine the grip size you need.

Finally, you may notice a line of arrows running the length of a grip. These have been placed there to help you maintain correct alignment when you grip the club.

The Shaft   The shaft of the golf club is usually made of steel but may be made of fiberglass, graphite, boron, or composite materials. Shafts vary in weight and flex. Some of the newer materials, such as graphite and boron, are thought to be more forgiving and provide more power. The shafts bend a little during the swing and snap forward as you are about to hit the ball. The newer materials are also lighter. A lighter shaft allows more weight in the clubhead, which, in turn, allows greater clubhead speed, thus more distance. The selection of a shaft is one of the most important elements in getting clubs that are appropriate for you.

Shaft Flex   Shaft **flex** is the tendency for the shaft to bend during the swing. In general, the shaft flex of your clubs should be appropriate for your size and strength. Stronger people can usually move the clubhead faster. The faster one can move the clubhead, the stiffer the shaft flex should be. Men's clubs generally have a regular shaft flex (R flex), which is appropriate for most men, and a stiff shaft flex (S flex), which is recommended only for younger, stronger men, particularly those with some experience playing the sport. Women's clubs generally have an R flex shaft, which is recommended for stronger women players, and an A flex shaft, which is more flexible and appropriate for most women. In general, women players should avoid S flex clubs. Senior players of both sexes should usually select the more flexible A flex shaft.

Club Weight   Appropriate club weight is determined by your body size, strength, and swing characteristics. Club weight is based on the overall weight of the club and the weight of the clubhead. Clubs should have enough weight in the clubhead to give you "feel" during the swing. If too much weight is in the grip and shaft, the clubhead is difficult to control precisely.

Club Lie   The **club lie** is the angle between the clubhead and the ground (Figure 2-4). The ideal club lie varies with the height of the golfer. A club has the proper lie if the clubhead is flat on the ground when you **address** the ball (that is, when you ground the club in preparation for hitting the ball) and neither the heel nor toe of the club is elevated. The proper club lie should allow you to address the ball comfortably without bending over too much or standing too upright. Club lie is one of the most important features of your clubs—perhaps even more important than club length.

Clubhead Back   Clubheads are categorized as either **cavity-back** or **muscle-back** (Figure 2-5). In the traditional muscle-back clubs, the weight is concentrated in the center of the clubhead (called the "sweet spot"). Cavity-back clubs have weight taken out of the back of the club and concentrated on the sole, heel, and toe of the clubhead. These clubs are more forgiving. If a ball is hit slightly off-center, the club has enough weight in its outer parts to perform a good shot. An off-center shot like this twists the cavity-back clubhead less than it does the muscle-back clubhead. With muscle-back clubs, you must hit the ball in the center of the club face (the sweet spot) because that's where the weight of the club is centered. These clubs are less forgiving of off-center shots.

Irons, woods, and putters are all now made with cavity backs. As with irons, cavity-back woods and putters allow you to hit a shot slightly off the club's sweet spot and still make a good shot. Today, cavity-back clubs are far more popular than muscle-back

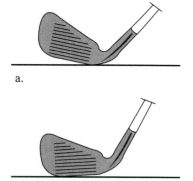

a.

b.

Figure 2-4

(a) Improper club lie. (b) Proper club lie. The clubhead is flat on the ground when you address the ball; neither the heel nor toe of the club is elevated.

clubs. However, many professional golfers prefer the traditional clubs. They have the skill to hit the sweet spot more consistently than the average golfer.

Woods Traditionally, the clubheads of **woods** were made of persimmon or laminated maple, which is how the clubs got their names. Although many of these clubs are still made of wood, clubheads constructed of lightweight steel or carbon fiber are the materials of choice for most amateur and professional golfers these days. Metal woods are easy to maintain, and most golfers feel they are easier to hit than the more traditional wood clubs.

In the past, woods had strange names like brassie (2-wood), spoon (3-wood), and cleek (4-wood). Now, like irons, woods are classified by number. The 1-wood is called the **driver,** and the other woods are often called "fairway woods." The higher the number of the wood, the greater the loft. Loft is the angle of the club face. It determines the trajectory of the ball after it is hit by the club. Like irons, woods with a higher number hit the ball higher in the air, have shorter shafts, and are easier to control. Woods 1–5 are the most common in the golfer's arsenal, but one club manufacturer even makes a 15-wood. Wood 6 or 7—both of which are popular with women players—is a good alternative to using long irons and is easier for some golfers to control.

As with irons, consider grip size, shaft flex, swing weight, lie, and clubhead configurations when buying woods.

In general, you need only two or three woods in your bag. A good combination is a 1- and a 3-wood or 1-, 3-, and 5-woods.

Buying Your First Set of Clubs A reasonably good set of clubs costs a minimum of $300 (not including bag, head covers, etc.), and you can easily pay more than $1000 for a top quality set of irons and woods. A good set of clubs will last for many years, but for many beginning golfers—who don't know if they are still going to be playing the sport in 6 months, let alone in 10 years—there are better ways to go.

One strategy is to buy a good starter set of clubs at a reasonable price. If you get really hooked on the game, then you can purchase a good set of clubs that has been fitted to your size, strength, and playing ability. You can easily sell your starter set through the classified section of the newspaper.

Another excellent strategy, and one that I highly recommend, is to look for a used set of high-quality clubs. Golf clubs don't deteriorate very fast. Often, you can get an older set of top-of-the-line clubs at the same price as a new, poor-quality starter

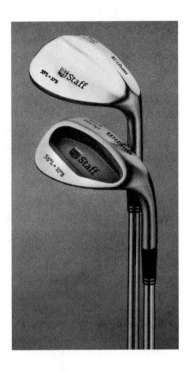

Figure 2-5
Clubheads.

set. Check the bulletin boards of golf courses and driving ranges as well as the local newspaper.

It's a good idea to try clubs out first—even when buying them off the shelf at the local sporting goods store. Many pro shops will let you borrow clubs to find out which type is best for you. You can even try the exact clubs you plan to buy; the pro will put tape over the club face so you don't scratch it. Try a variety of clubs so you can get a good feel for what you like. Many sports shops have nets that you can hit into as you try different clubs. This isn't as good as trying them on a course or driving range, but it's better than taking them from the box to the golf course.

When you are ready to buy a top-quality set of clubs, have an experienced professional determine the correct grip size, swing weight, club lie, and shaft flex. Take your time deciding. Good golf clubs are a big investment and can have a significant effect on how fast you learn and master the game. Remember, though, the most important factor in choosing clubs is how they feel to you. Unless they feel good, you won't be happy with them—regardless of cost.

Care of Your Golf Clubs   Golf clubs are much easier to maintain than they used to be. In the days of wooden shafts and laminated wooden clubheads, great care had to be given to the clubs to keep them from warping. Today's all-metal clubs are almost maintenance-free. All you need to do is keep them clean.

Clean the dirt and grass from the grooves on the club faces of metal woods and irons after you play. These grooves "bite" the ball and cause backspin, which is important for control of your shots. Clean the clubs with a short bristle brush available at any pro shop or sporting goods store.

The most vulnerable part of the clubs are the grips. Most golfers pay little attention to them, but they can easily loose their tackiness as they accumulate dirt and oils. Clean them regularly and have them replaced when they are no longer serviceable.

Wooden clubs also have to be properly maintained. Nicks and scratches can let moisture in, which will warp clubheads and change their playing characteristics. After you play, particularly on a wet day, let the clubs dry out naturally without the club covers on. Turn the club covers themselves inside out so they can dry out as well. After clubs and covers dry, put the covers back on and store the clubs in a cool dry place, such as a bedroom closet. Don't store your wooden clubs in a place where they will be subject to radical temperature changes. Periodically, take your clubs to a pro shop for refinishing.

Golf Bag

Your choice of golf bag depends on whether you are going to carry your clubs, pull them around with a hand cart, or use a motor-driven golf cart (Figure 2-6). Buy a light, simple bag if you plan to carry it around the course. Bags are made of many different materials, including canvas, synthetic fabrics, and leather. They range in cost from a low of about $20 to over $1000 for a fine leather bag.

If you plan on carrying your bag, it should be lightweight and have a supporting shaft down its length to make handling the clubs on the course easier. The carrying strap should be broad and padded enough so it doesn't cut into your shoulder. The bag should have at least one compartment for storing items such as spare balls, tees, and a score card. Some carry bags have built-in tripods that make the bag more manageable. With the tripod, you

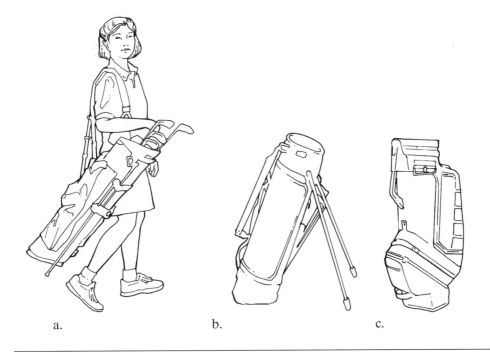

a.   b.   c.

Figure 2-6

Different style golf bags. (a) Get a lightweight bag if you plan to walk the course. (b) A bag with a built-in tripod makes it easier to get your clubs. (c) Heavier, larger bags are often preferred by people who drive a golf cart when they play.

don't have to lay your clubs on the ground, which protects them from damage and makes club selection easier.

Larger, heavier bags are made for people who drive a golf cart or pull their bag around in a hand cart. These bags are often very elaborate and have numerous compartments for carrying golf supplies, extra clothing, and snacks. If you plan to walk the course with one of these monsters, be sure you're in good shape— or be prepared for a major physical ordeal.

Hand carts are a good compromise for those who want some exercise while they play, yet want to avoid carrying their clubs. A cart is handy because it allows you ready access to your clubs, gives you a base on which to write your score, and easily stores extra balls and tees. Buy a good, sturdy golf cart that easily folds up into the trunk of your car.

Golf Balls

Golf ball specifications are spelled out in great detail in the rules. Advertisements for super balls are either not true or the balls are illegal. The only differences between different brands of golf balls are the quality of the materials, compressibility of the balls, and size of the dimples (dimples are the small holes on the surface of the golf ball). The most durable ball has a Surlyn cover. This ball is difficult to cut, so it is a good choice for beginners. Other balls use balata covers, which are thinner and less durable than Surlyn but spin more easily and are easier to control.

Golf balls have compressibility ratings of 80, 90, and 100. The higher the rating, the harder the ball has to be hit in order to compress it. The compressibility rating is not particularly important to a beginner, but if you hit the ball very hard, then a higher rating may be an advantage.

Dimple size affects the aerodynamics of the golf ball by providing lift. Balls with large dimples tend to go further when you are hitting with the wind but go shorter distances when you are hitting against the wind. Again, for the beginning golfer, dimple size is not particularly important.

Shoes

Golf shoes are a must for any serious golfer. Good golf shoes should be comfortable and lightweight; they should keep your feet dry and allow them to breathe (get rid of excess water vapor); and they should provide support. Golf shoes come in a variety of styles ranging from the traditional kiltie style (a **kiltie** is a leather flap attached to the front of a golf shoe; see Figure 2-7) to those that

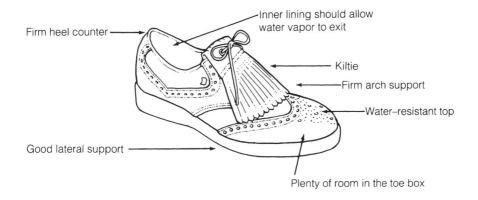

Firm heel counter

Inner lining should allow water vapor to exit

Kiltie

Firm arch support

Water–resistant top

Good lateral support

Plenty of room in the toe box

Figure 2-7

Golf shoe with kiltie. Good golf shoes should be comfortable and lightweight, should keep your feet dry, and should provide support.

resemble jogging shoes. Your choice depends on what you consider fashionable and how much walking you plan to do. If you are walking the course, buy shoes you can walk in for four hours without getting sore feet and blisters.

Support is very important in golf. If you slip during a swing, your shot will not be accurate. To avoid slipping, metal spiked shoes are the best, but rubber spikes are also popular. Avoid the Astroturf kind of shoes worn by football players and coaches because they can damage the greens. Make sure your shoes provide good lateral support as well.

Golf Glove

A golf glove is beneficial because it helps you maintain a good grip and prevents blisters (Figure 2-8). Most good golfers wear a glove for all shots, including putting. The golf glove is generally worn on your control hand, which is the left hand if you are right-handed (and vice versa). The glove is usually made of leather and should be large enough to cover your entire palm—but not so big as to allow the club to move during your swing. A good glove should be durable, facilitate ventilation, repel water, and have a Velcro closure to ensure snugness. Most golf gloves include a ball marker disguised to look like a button.

Clothing

Golf is a fairly formal game, and the majority of courses have dress codes. Many courses will not allow you to play wearing tank tops,

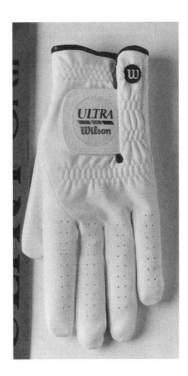

Figure 2-8

Golf glove. A golf glove helps you maintain a good grip and prevents blisters.

jogging shorts, or tennis shoes. You will save yourself embarrassment if you inquire about the dress code of a course before playing.

Pants and Shorts   Men and women can wear shorts (no shorter than 19 inches) or pants, and women can wear golf skirts. These items are generally made of cotton or a cotton-polyester blend. They should not be so tight that they are uncomfortable or so loose that they interfere with the golf swing.

Shirts   In general, shirts should have sleeves and collars, but women are often allowed to wear sleeveless shirts. Like pants and shorts, the best golf shirts are made of cotton or cotton-polyester blends. Sleeves should be slightly longer than normal to protect you from the sun, and the ends should be loose enough to allow freedom of movement. The shirt should be roomy but not so big that it interferes with your swing.

Miscellaneous Supplies: Ball Retriever, Scorecard, Pencil, Tees, and Ball Marker

A ball retriever, a collapsible pole with a cup or basket on the end, is a useful device for recovering balls that are only slightly out of reach in water. The retriever keeps you from getting wet.

Scorecards are available free of charge at the golf course. They contain a variety of useful information, such as distances of holes, relative difficulty, and local rules and should be studied carefully before and during the round. Figure 2-9 shows the elements of a scorecard. The distance for each hole is shown for the blue, white, gold, and red tees. The blue tee, or **championship tee,** is the longest distance. This tee is generally played in golf tournaments or by more skilled golfers, but anyone can play from the championship tee—it is simply more difficult to get a good score. The standard tees used by the USGA are the back tee, middle tee, and forward tee. Some golf courses indicate by handicap which tee a golfer should use, and some courses have an additional, shorter tee that may be appropriate for seniors, children, or beginners.

Par is the number of strokes an expert player is expected to take to complete a hole. Par assumes two putts for each hole. Thus, on a par 4 hole, an expert is expected to take two strokes to reach the green and two strokes to putt the ball into the hole. A **birdie** is one stroke below par, and an **eagle** is two strokes below par. If you get the ball into the hole from the tee in only one stroke, you have scored a **hole-in-one,** or an **ace.** One stroke over par is called a **bogey,** two strokes over par is a double bogey,

Scorer									Date				Attest								
HOLE	1	2	3	4	5	6	7	8	9	OUT	10	11	12	13	14	15	16	17	18	IN	TOTAL
BLUE TEE	430	540	172	402	390	206	590	395	390	3515	405	348	334	188	525	183	450	371	578	3382	6897
WHITE TEE	398	520	130	369	356	181	562	375	362	3253	380	330	314	162	489	122	376	359	552	3084	6337
HANDICAP HOLES	5	3	17	13	11	15	1	9	7		8	14	16	10	2	18	12	6	4		
PAR	4	5	3	4	4	3	5	4	4	36	4	4	4	3	5	3	4	4	5	36	72
+/-																					
GOLD TEE	383	486	128	350	345	161	520	359	346	3078	343	330	314	150	465	102	344	307	510	2865	5943
RED TEE	348	475	125	325	333	151	485	332	322	2896	312	305	286	135	445	78	321	307	406	2595	5491

Figure 2-9
The scorecard.

and so forth. Double and triple bogeys are very common among beginners. As your skills improve, you will get more pars and birdies and fewer bogeys.

"Handicap Holes" refers to the relative difficulty of each of the holes. On this course, the 562-yard, par 5 7th hole is considered the most difficult, while the 122-yard, par 3 15th hole is rated easiest. "Out" and "In" refer to your score for the first and second nine holes, respectively.

Handicap refers to your rating as a golfer, which is established with the USGA. Your handicap is the average number of strokes you shoot above par. A player who shoots an average score of 90 on a par 72 course will have a handicap of 18 (90 − 72 = 18). The highest handicap a player can have is 36 for men and 40 for women; the lowest is zero. Handicaps allow players of different abilities to compete against each other more fairly.

Other supplies you will need on the course include a pencil, tees, and a ball marker. Pencils are available free of charge at the clubhouse. Tees are available at the pro shop, either free or at a minimal charge. Tees are made of wood or plastic and should be solid enough to hold the ball without falling over. Try to avoid plastic tees, however, because they can damage your woods. Ball markers are used to mark where your ball is on the green and may be a small button with a plastic spike on the bottom, a coin, or the buttonlike marker attached to many golf gloves.

FINDING A PLACE TO PRACTICE

Practice is the key to becoming a good golfer. A driving range, either at a golf course or a separate establishment, is probably the best place to hone your skills. Try to find a range that lets you hit from grass tees because these will feel more like what you will encounter on the golf course. Ranges that use rubber mats and tees, although better than nothing, provide much different conditions than you see during a real game. Most driving ranges have facilities for practicing putting, chipping, and bunker shots.

You can also practice in any open grassy field. Although many schools and recreation departments will not allow golfers to practice on their fields because of safety considerations, there are plenty of other fields around. Buy a golf ball shag bag, which helps you pick up balls without bending over, from a local sporting goods store, and you will be able to practice anytime the field is vacant.

A home net is another practice alternative. You can purchase a home golf net for about $300. It allows you to work on your game anytime of the day or night (if your family will put up with it!). One problem with golf nets is that you can't see what happened to your shot—it may not be obvious in a net whether you hit a slice or a hook. Using whiffle balls is another excellent alternative for home practice.

For putting, try to practice on a real putting green as much as possible. However, you can also practice putting at home with a portable golf hole you can set up on your living room carpet. Putting on your rug will help you develop touch that will carry over to the golf course. Many golf courses have practice greens. During a lunch hour or for a few minutes before going home from work or school, stop at the course and practice your chipping and putting. There is typically no charge for using the facility.

PLAYING A GOLF COURSE FOR THE FIRST TIME

After you have taken some lessons and developed some skill on the practice range, it's time to put yourself to the test on a golf course. It's probably best to start with a nine-hole executive course. These courses cater to the beginner. Although they consist mainly of par 3 holes of less than 150 yards, they often have one or two par 4's as well. Before you play any golf course, be sure you understand basic etiquette and the rules of golf so you don't offend other golfers (see Chapter 6).

You will need to reserve a **tee time**—even on a nine-hole course. Call the starter and tell him or her what time you would like to play and the number of people in your party. Players are sent around the course in groups of four or less. If you are by yourself, you will be paired with other golfers, unless there are few people playing that day.

Arrive at the course in plenty of time to pay your greens fees and warm up properly. If there is no driving range at the course, you may wish to stop at one before going on to the golf course to play. After warming up, get a score card and study the layout of the course. Periodically, the starter will call out the party on the tee and the parties to follow. You can expect a five to ten minute wait between parties, so be ready to tee off when your name is called.

Playing 18 Holes for the First Time

Golfers at standard 18-hole courses tend to be more serious and skilled than those who play nine-hole courses. However, many golfers on the larger course will not be much better than you, so you shouldn't become overly intimidated. The procedure for playing an 18-hole course is the same as for a nine-hole course: Reserve a tee time, report to the starter and pay your greens fees, report to the tee when your party is called. The first few times you play an 18-hole course, it's probably a good idea to play with a friend who is an experienced golfer. This will help you avoid embarrassing mistakes and decrease your anxiety.

The course you choose may be a public course owned by the local government, a privately owned course open to the public, or a private course, open only to members. To play courses open to the public, you need only reserve a tee time and pay the greens fees. To play a private club, you must be invited by a member. Private clubs have some of the nicest golf courses in the world. It is often very expensive to join and it may take approval from the membership for you to be accepted as a member. However, in the United States and Canada, there are many places to play golf without having to join a private club.

If you walk and carry your clubs, playing 18 holes of golf can be tiring. A typical golf game takes four to five hours—make sure you're in good condition before playing 18 holes for the first time. Conditioning for golf is discussed in Chapter 7.

Worksheet

1. The basic equipment you need to play golf includes _____,
   _____, _____.

2. What is the maximum number of clubs you can carry in your golf bag during a game? _____

3. The longer the iron, the longer the _____
   length and steeper the angle of the _____.

4. _____ irons tend to hit the ball further and at a lower trajectory than _____ irons.

5. Name the three parts of a golf club: _____, _____, _____.

6. The three basic club flexes are _____, _____, _____.

7. _____ clubs have weight taken out of the back of the club and concentrated
   on the sole, heel, and toe of the club head.

8. The number of strokes that an expert player is expected to take to complete a hole is called
   _____.

9. Your _____ is the average number of strokes you shoot above par. It is
   your rating as a golfer and is established with the USGA.

10. You have scored a _____ when you have shot one stroke under par.

11. You have scored a _____ when you have shot one stroke over par.

Mastering the Basics

Playing well consistently is a matter of mastering the basic movements of the swing. The golf swing is the same for most strokes; that is, you swing a driver from the tee in the same way you would an 8-iron from the fairway. The basics include grip, stance, backswing, forward swing, and follow-through. If you become proficient in these elements, you will have made significant progress toward becoming a good golfer.

Golf magazines and books are full of advice about how to change subtle aspects of your swing—forget them for now. Until you have mastered the basics, these minor points are just that: minor. For example, golf pros sometimes discuss the best place to break the wrist during the swing—gradually during the backswing or more abruptly at the top of the swing. Although this is important, it is of little consequence if you move your head radically during the swing or grip the club incorrectly. Again, learn the basics and you will have gone a long way toward mastering this game.

To master the golf swing, you must become increasingly proficient in two aspects of the movement that sometimes work against each other: accuracy and power. Accuracy results mainly from maintaining proper alignment between the clubhead and ball. Power comes from coordinating the actions of the legs, hips, torso, arms, and hands to develop clubhead velocity.

If you were to perform the swing in slow motion and stop the club when it reached the ball, you could easily align the ball and

25

the clubhead in the same position as when you started the swing. But, of course, things are not so simple. During a normal swing, generating power and maintaining alignment between the club and ball requires that you coordinate the movement of your ankles, knees, hips, spine, shoulders, elbows, wrists, and neck. Nevertheless, if you keep the movement as simple as possible, trying to generate the most power with the least effort, you can develop a consistent, powerful golf swing.

THE GRIP

The grip is critical to maintaining proper alignment between the ball and the clubhead. Your grip should be tight enough to keep the club aligned in your hand during the swing but loose enough to ensure that the swing is smooth and fluid. Most beginning golfers grip the club too tightly. Control and power in the grip come from the fingers rather than the palms. You must become comfortable with the proper grip from the start.

Many professional golfers use variations on the basic grip. However, they have to compensate for their grip in other aspects of their swing. Such compensation may be difficult for the average recreational golfer. Again, keep your game simple and you will be successful. The proper grip for left- and right-handed players is shown in Figure 3-1a and b. Your fingers, rather than your palms, control the club, so finger position is critical. Note that instructions in this book are for right-handed players; left-handed players should generally do the reverse.

A good way to think about the grip is to think of yourself as "shaking hands" with the club, pointing your thumbs down the shaft. Your hands should work as a unit. The grip should be firm but not tight.

Top Hand

For right-handed players, the left hand is on top; for left-handed players, the right hand is on top. Stand in a comfortable position and address the ball by aligning the clubface with the intended target. You are usually trying to hit the ball straight, so the clubface should be perpendicular to a line between the target and ball. Start with your hands and arms hanging at your sides naturally. Place the club handle in your top hand so it rests in a line between the base of the little finger and the middle of first segment of the index finger (Figure 3-2a, b). The end of the club should extend about ¼-inch beyond the heel of your open hand. Allow your

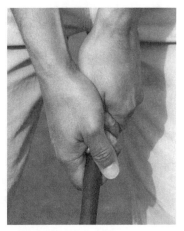
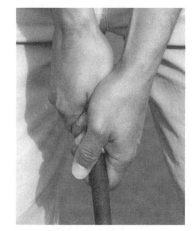

a. Right-handed golfer   b. Left-handed golfer

Figure 3-1

Proper grip for right-handed and left-handed golfers. "Shake hands" with the club, pointing your thumbs down the shaft. Your hands should work as a unit. The grip should be firm but not tight.

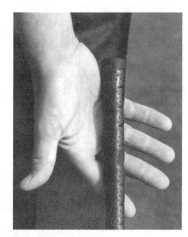

a. Right-handed golfer   b. Left-handed golfer

Figure 3-2

Position of top hand for right- and left-handed golfers, with hand open. Right-handed golfers place left hand on top; left-handed golfers place the right hand on top.

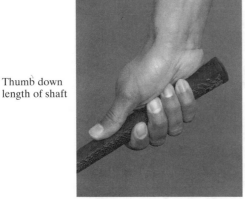

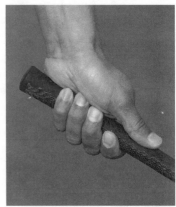

Thumb down
length of shaft

Top of the grip ¼ inch
above heal of hand

Pressure on last three
fingers

a. Right-handed golfer

b. Left-handed golfer

Figure 3-3
Position of top hand for right- and left-handed golfers, with hand
closed.

thumb to close over the top of the club so that it is turned slightly
to the right side of the handle (left side for left-handed players)
(Figure 3-3a, b). The fleshy part of the palm near the little finger
helps stabilize the grip, but most of the pressure exerted by the top
hand comes from the last three fingers (middle, ring, and little
fingers). These fingers must hold the club against the palm firmly
enough (remember, firm but not tight) so the club doesn't turn in
your hands during the swing. In the meantime, the thumb and
forefinger, which do not exert much pressure, are important in
guiding the club during the swing.

Bottom Hand

For right-handed golfers, the right hand is on the bottom; for left-
handed golfers, the left hand is on the bottom. Place your right
(left) index finger squarely against the side of the club with your
palm facing toward the target and your thumb placed down the
shaft, slightly on the left (right) side of the grip (that is, at 11
o'clock on the face of the club for right-handed golfers and at 1
o'clock for left-handed players) (Figures 3-4, 3-5, 3-6). Let your
fingers grasp the club naturally, so it rests across the base of the
first segment of the index finger and across the joint at the base of
the little finger. The middle and ring fingers of the bottom hand

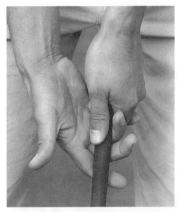

a. Right-handed golfer   b. Left-handed golfer

Figure 3-4

Position of bottom hand for right- and left-handed golfers, with
hand open. Right-handed golfers place right hand on the bottom,
left-handed golfers place the left hand on the bottom.

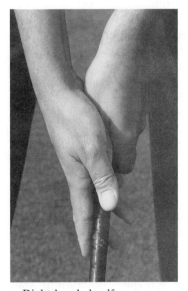
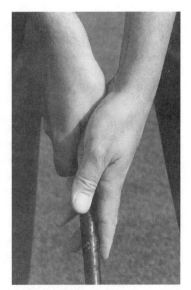

a. Right-handed golfer   b. Left-handed golfer

Figure 3-5

The right hand (left hand for left-handed players) is placed
squarely against the side of the club.

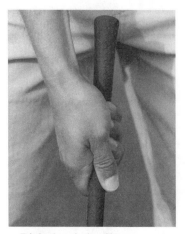 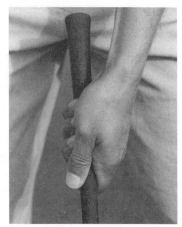

a. Right-handed golfer   b. Left-handed golfer

Figure 3-6

Position of bottom hand for right- and left-handed golfers, with hand closed.

exert most of the pressure. Although all fingers exert some pressure, be sure the thumb of the bottom hand exerts very little. This is important for maintaining control of the clubhead and preventing the bottom hand from becoming dominant during the swing. A dominant thumb may close the club face (cause it to turn inward) and cause the ball to hook.

Link Between Left and Right Hands

The ideal grip should allow the hands to function as a unit. To accomplish this, the hands should overlap or interlock (Figure 3-7). In the **overlapping,** or **Vardon, grip** (Harry Vardon was a great golfer from around the turn of the century), the little finger of the right hand overlaps the left hand between the index and middle finger. This grip is the recommended one, and it's used by most golfers. In the **interlocking grip,** the little finger of the right hand wraps around the index finger of the left hand. A third variation is the **10-finger grip** (sometimes called the "baseball grip"), in which there is no linkage between the hands. This last grip is seldom used but is favored by some golfers who have trouble rotating or releasing the club face when hitting the ball.

Notice that as your hands grip the club, the thumb and forefinger of each hand form a V. If you are holding the club correctly,

  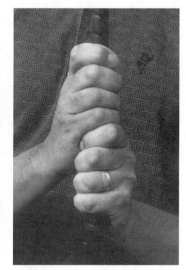

a. Overlapping grip   b. Interlocking grip   c. 10-Finger (baseball) grip

Figure 3-7
Three methods of linking right and left hands: overlapping grip, interlocking grip, and 10-finger (baseball) grip.

the base of each V should be pointing to about the area between your chin and your right shoulder (left shoulder for left-handed players).

Some players prefer a grip slightly stronger or weaker than the neutral grip, in which the hand position is between a strong and weak grip (Figure 3-8). In a strong grip, the bottom hand drops under the club, and the V of the bottom hand drops below the right shoulder (left shoulder for left-handed players). In the weaker grip, the bottom hand moves over the top of the club.

The grip is the foundation of a good swing. It ensures that you can swing the club on the correct path and properly align the club face to the ball at impact. Use the correct grip and practice it until it feels natural during your swing.

THE ADDRESS POSITION

The Stance

Your **stance** is the platform from which you hit the ball. A good stance puts you in good balance and allows you to apply full force

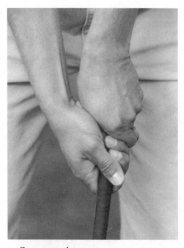 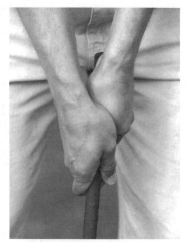

a. Strong grip   b. Weak grip

Figure 3-8

Strong and weak grips. Right-handed players turn the right hand to the right to strengthen the grip and to the left to weaken it. Left-handed players do the opposite.

to the ball as you hit it. A good stance contributes to accuracy and consistency because it allows you more easily to swing the same way every time you hit the ball.

The stance in golf, as in most sports, puts you in the basic athletic position (Figure 3-9a, b): weight firmly and evenly distributed over both feet, with the center of gravity running up the midline of the body. This position allows you to move your weight easily and naturally to your back foot during the back swing and forward to your front foot during the forward swing.

The golf stance should place you in a natural, comfortable position with feet placed about shoulders width apart (Figure 3-10). Bend your knees and hips slightly. Distribute your weight evenly between your feet. Let your arms extend naturally so you are not cramped or reaching when you address the ball. Your right shoulder should be slightly below your left (reverse for left-handed players). Your arms and the club form a y that you must maintain when striking the ball. As you swing, your hands should be slightly ahead of the ball and angled slightly toward the inside of the front thigh.

The relative positions of the ball and your front and back feet depend on the club you're using (the front foot is the one closest to

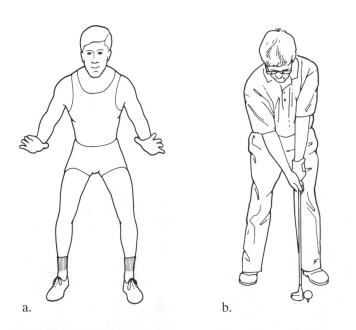

a.   b.

Figure 3-9

Basic athletic position. (a) In the basic athletic position, the knees
are bent, feet provide firm support, and the spine is properly
aligned. (b) The golfer uses these same elements when addressing
the ball.

Figure 3-10

The golf stance. Place your
feet approximately shoul-
ders' width apart. Narrow
your stance slightly as you
progress through shorter
clubs. Lean forward from
the hips, flex your knees,
and keep your back straight.

the place where you want to hit the ball). When you are using a
driver, use a square stance, with toes squarely aligned and the ball
aligned with the inside of your front heel (Figure 3-11a). In general, avoid a closed stance, in which the front foot is closer than the
back foot to the target line (an imaginary line between the ball and
the target, usually the hole), because it can lead to pushed,
hooked, and **fat shots.**

As you move to shorter irons (8-iron to wedge), move the ball
back a little, open your stance, and move your feet together
slightly. You are in an open stance when your front foot is further
from the ball than the back foot (Figure 3-11b). To get into an open
stance, align the toes of your front foot with the middle of your
back foot. The open stance is better for shorter irons because it
makes your swing arc in a more outward and upward direction,
which causes the club face to strike the ball at a downward angle
and makes the ball fly higher in the air.

a. Square stance   b. Open stance

Figure 3-11

Square and open stances. (a) In the square stance, the toes are parallel and the ball is aligned with the front heel. (b) In the open stance, the front foot is placed behind the rear foot and the ball is moved back (compared to the square stance).

Alignment

Alignment is critical in hitting the ball where you want it to go. You should be able to draw a line between your toes or hips or shoulders that is parallel to the target line; this is called "parallel-left" alignment (because you are aligned to the left of the target; substitute "right" if you're a left-handed player). A good technique for determining correct alignment is to place a club on the

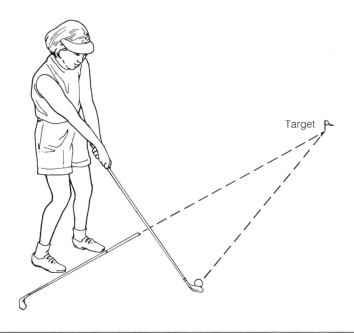

Target

Figure 3-12

Using a golf club to determine proper alignment. Place a club on
the ground in a line parallel to your toes. If the club points to the
target, you are properly aligned.

ground in a line parallel to your toes (Figure 3-12). If the club
points to the target, you are properly aligned. On the course, you
can do this more easily by holding the club at waist level and point
it at the target. Align your feet so they are parallel with the imaginary line between the club and the target.

Another good technique for establishing alignment is to use a
focal point called an intermediate target. Pick an object, such as a
broken tee or clump of grass, that is in line with the ball and the
target. It is easier to line up with a target that is close to you rather
than one that is 150 yards or more from you. Stand so you are
parallel to the imaginary line between the ball, the object, and the
target (Figure 3-13).

The position of the club face is also critical to alignment. Before starting your swing, check to make sure the club face is per-

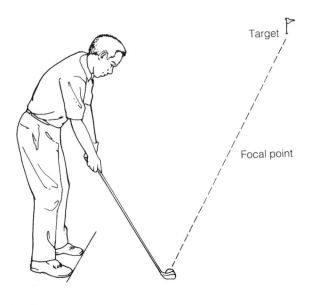

Target

Focal point

Figure 3-13

Using a focal point to determine proper alignment. Pick an object
that is in line with the ball and the target. Stand so you are parallel
to the imaginary line between the ball, the object, and the target.

pendicular to the line between the ball and the target. If you align
your club face properly when you address the ball, you have a
better chance of making the ball go straight.

The Waggle

Before starting the back swing, most golfers do a waggle with their
club. A **waggle** is a small forward and backward movement of the
club, performed primarily with the wrist, that's done before starting the swing. It's similar to tennis players bouncing a ball on the
court before serving. There are many explanations for why a
golfer waggles, such as it relaxes the golfer before he or she
swings, helps set up rhythm, and creates "positive muscle" memory for causing forward movement of the ball. From a mechanical
standpoint, there is no obvious reason for including a waggle in

your golf swing—but it probably won't hurt, so do it if you feel the need (just don't overdo it because it holds up play).

Maintaining the Center of Rotation

Maintaining the center of rotation is the most important aspect of the stance and swing. Your swing should revolve around the center of your sternum (breast bone) or around an imaginary line running up the middle of your chest (midline). One important cause of moving outside the center of rotation is trying to hit the ball too hard. Doing so moves your head and torso forward or to the left during the transfer of weight from the right foot to the left foot. Try to relax and let the club do the work.

Your head should be stationary during the swing except for its rotational movement (see Figure 3-14a, b, c). A good practice is to align your left eye (right for left-handed players) over the ball, which helps keep your head steady. During the golf swing, the

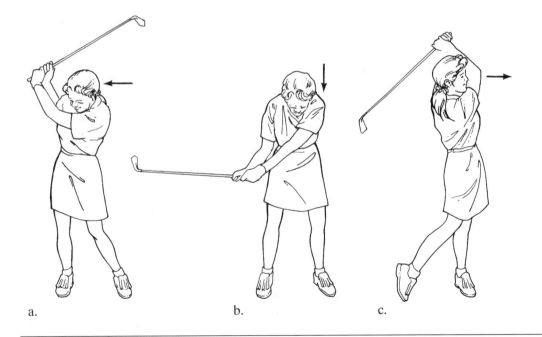

a.   b.   c.

Figure 3-14
Typical head movement errors (some head movement is normal):
(a) excessive backward head movement during backswing, (b) excessive downward movement during downswing, (c) excessive forward head movement during downswing.

head will rotate a little to the right and then a little to the left. It is also pulled around in response to the motion of the forward swing. However, try to avoid excessive head movement. Moving the body outside the center of rotation is the single most widespread cause of bad shots. When you move outside the center of rotation, it is difficult to return to the exact position from which you initially addressed the ball.

Beginning golfers have a tendency to raise their head as they progress through the swing so they can see where the ball went. This almost invariably causes **topping** (hitting the upper part of the ball), which causes the ball to be hit on the ground, usually a short distance.

THE BACKSWING

After proper grip and maintaining the center of rotation during the swing, a good backswing is the most important factor in making consistently good shots. The backswing determines the arc and tempo of the shot. As we have seen, a well-executed golf swing involves coordinating the movement of all major joints in the body. A good backswing helps ensure that during the forward swing the lower and upper body will work together, giving you the greatest degree of control and power as you contact the ball.

Recall that when you address the ball, with hands slightly ahead of it, your arms and club form an imaginary y. Maintain this y during the early stage of the backswing (during the first two feet). The backswing involves slowly and smoothly moving your hands and arms backward as you turn your shoulders (Figure 3-15a, b). Think of the movement as a "one-piece" takeaway, with all your body segments "connected." Turn your hips slightly in the direction of the backswing during the takeaway. This eases trunk rotation during the swing, helps make the swing arc wide, and helps you shift your weight properly during the forward part of the swing. The arc is the path your club follows during the swing. Try to make the arc of the backswing and forward swing the same. The movement of the hands, arms, and shoulders occurs as a single, coordinated movement. Keep the wrists firm as you begin the backswing—otherwise, the hands and arms will tend to dominate the swing. A good backswing allows proper weight shift, a good turning motion with the shoulders, and a proper arc during your swing.

A good shoulder turn is important for good power (Figure 3-15c, d). At the end of the backswing, the back of the right shoulder should be pointing at the target. At the top of the swing, the

a. Right-handed golfer   b. Left-handed golfer

c. Right-handed golfer   d. Left-handed golfer

Figure 3-15

The backswing. Hands and arms move backward and shoulders
turn in a single, coordinated movement.

clubhead and hands should be high (the shaft of the club should be approximately horizontal to the ground), with the clubhead pointing toward the target. This position should occur naturally as a result of a proper backswing rather than from a conscious effort to raise your hands and club.

A full shoulder turn requires good flexibility in the trunk and spine. You will develop flexibility in these areas by playing golf and doing proper exercises. Principles for developing flexibility and fitness for golf are given in Chapter 7.

During the turn, your left heel should not lift far from the ground. Let your feet roll naturally during the backswing and forward swing. These subtle foot movements will help you transfer your weight during the swing.

You will break your wrist at some point during the backswing. Two techniques are to break them gradually and smoothly throughout the backswing or break them abruptly at the top of the swing. Either technique is acceptable. However, don't break them at the beginning of the swing. Doing so will encourage you to lead the swing with your hands rather than with your hands, arms, and shoulders as a unit. Maintain the unit formed by your hands, wrists, arms, and shoulders until your hands are about waist high.

Arc of the Backswing

The arc of the swing is partially determined by the club you use. With a driver, the arc will be flatter; with a short iron, it will be more upright. The swing should follow a continuous arc, much like the hub of a wheel (Figure 3-16). If you keep your hands within the arc, turn your shoulders sufficiently, and keep your left arm straight during the swing, you will achieve a good swing arc and make more consistent shots. Maintaining a good center of rotation also helps you achieve the proper swing arc. A smooth arc ensures that you will strike the ball at the same position as when you first addressed it.

THE FORWARD SWING

The forward swing, or downswing, is easy if you set yourself up well during the backswing. Begin the forward swing with a movement from the hips—as if they are turning in a barrel—followed almost immediately by the legs, arms, and shoulders moving together (Figure 3-17). Try to maintain the same arc you followed during the backswing (see Figure 3-16). If you begin the forward

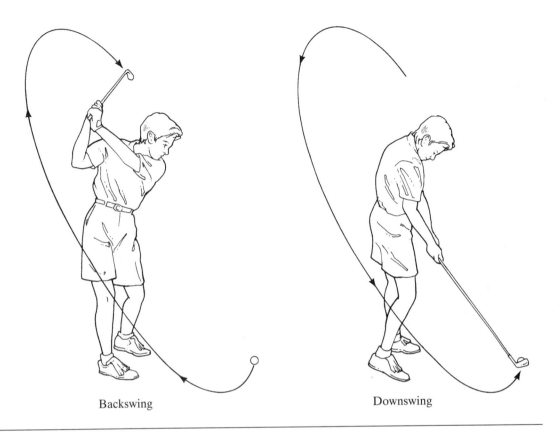

Backswing   Downswing

Figure 3-16
The arc of the downswing should be very close to the arc of the
backswing.

swing with your legs, maintaining the same arc is easier than it is if
the hands dominate the beginning of the movement. Leading the
forward swing with your hands or shoulders causes you to deviate
from an ideal arc and results in your hitting across the ball, causing
a hook or slice.

The left side of the body dominates the forward swing. It is
critical that the left arm remain straight during this part of the
swing and that the head remain still. During the forward swing, the
left arm gradually rotates outward so the club face addresses the
ball squarely at impact. It is critical that you maintain the y as you
contact the ball (Figure 3-18). Break your wrists only after contact.
A well-executed forward swing should "restore the radius." The
left arm, club shaft, and club face are returned to the same

Figure 3-17
The legs should initiate the downswing.

position as when you addressed the ball. Maintaining the y helps you correctly perform this critical aspect of the forward swing.

THE FOLLOW-THROUGH

Why worry about follow-through if the club has already hit the ball? A good **follow-through** is a result of a smoothly executed stroke (Figure 3-19). People with a choppy follow-through are hitting at the ball instead of through it. Think of the stroke as one continuous fluid motion. Don't get too hung up on the various segments of the swing or you will look like a robot on the tee.

In a properly executed follow-through, your hands should be higher than your head, with both arms to the side of the head (arms to the left side of the head if you're right-handed and vice versa if left-handed). (Notice in Figure 3–19 that the golfer is not

a.   b.

Figure 3-18

Maintain the y formation
of arms and club as you
make contact with the
ball. Do not break your
wrists prematurely.

Figure 3-19

A good follow-through is a consequence of a smoothly executed
swing. (a) Your weight should be on your front foot, rear heel
should be lifted, hips should be square to the target, and hands
should finish high. (b) Golfers who have back trouble should avoid
hyperextending the back during the follow-through.

looking down the fairway between her arms.) Weight should be on
your front foot with your hips squared to the front. Your rear knee
should be bent, with your toe pointed toward the ground.

DEVELOPING A FEEL FOR THE SWING

The basic elements of the golf swing have been described in this
chapter. Although it's important to remember these elements,
dwelling on them individually will make your movements overly
mechanical. Develop a sense of what a good swing feels like.
Avoid developing a mental checklist when you play—that is,
when you are about to swing, avoid saying to yourself, "Front arm
straight, eye on the ball, head steady, shift my weight, follow
through." Develop a sense of the swing where the elements of the
movement are integrated into a continuous, smooth motion.

Relax and Swing Easy

Many beginning golfers swing too hard. They attempt to rush the forward swing using their hands in the mistaken belief that it adds power to their swing. However, a swing that starts with the legs, arms, and shoulders moving together uses large, powerful muscles in a coordinated manner that generates plenty of power.

To avoid or correct this problem, consciously try to swing at 80 percent effort. This doesn't mean you should cut off the shoulder turn on your backswing. It means you should perform a full swing, but without trying so hard. Let your legs do the work. It may not feel like it, but you develop much more power this way than if you try to crank the ball using your upper body.

Faulty club selection also causes "overhitting." Instead of trying to hit a 7-iron as hard as you can, try hitting a 5- or 6-iron and take a relaxed swing. Although it is somewhat more difficult to hit a longer iron, there is not much actual difference between a 7-iron and a 6- or 5-iron. Also, unless a hole is a par 3, you have little chance of hitting the green from the tee, so relax and let your clubs get the distance for you.

It's better to be too relaxed than too tight. Tight muscles make your movements jerky and mechanical. If you're relaxed, your movements will be more fluid and powerful. A relaxed swing encourages you to develop a perception of what a good swing feels like. Rather than swinging at the ball, try to think of it as merely a position in your swing arc. You want to swing through the ball rather than at it.

Visualize and Think Positively

Visualization and positive thinking are discussed in Chapter 8. These concepts are critical for developing a fluid swing. On every shot, think positively. Positive thinking helps you swing more easily and without anxiety; negative thinking does the opposite. Think "This is going to be a great shot!" rather than "I know I'm going to duff the ball into the lake!"

Visualization helps you develop a feel for a smooth, effortless, successful swing. Use it every time you address the ball.

COMMON PROBLEMS WITH THE GOLF SWING

At some point, you will want to try various remedies for golf's big problems: slices, hooks, hitting the ball fat (hitting behind the ball), and topping the ball. Common problems with the golf swing and suggested remedies are shown in Table 3-1. Before you work

TABLE 3-1
Common Problems with the Golf Swing

PROBLEM	CAUSE	REMEDY
Swinging too hard	■ Attempting to initiate down-swing with upper body.	■ Initiate downswing with lower body. ■ Swing at 80% effort.
Bending the left elbow	■ Moving the clubhead back with the hands during the backswing	■ Don't move the left arm without moving shouders.
Slice (curved flight from left to right of the golfer)	■ Spin on the ball caused by hitting it with an open club face ■ Swing arc moving from out-side to inside during down-swing ■ Moving the head to the right	■ Hit ball with more of a closed club face. Rotate forearms counterclockwise during downswing. ■ Initiate downswing with legs. Maintain same swing arc during backswing and down-swing. ■ Keep head still; initiate downswing with the legs.
Hook (curved flight from right to left of the golfer)	■ Moving head to the left ■ Closing club face on contact with ball ■ Swing arc moving from out-side to inside during down-swing with closed club face	■ Swing around head and initi-ate downswing with the legs. ■ Improper grip. Right hand too far under grip (strong grip); correct grip. ■ Moving past ball on impact due to improperly starting downswing with upper body; start downswing with lower body.
Hitting the ball fat (hitting be-hind the ball)	■ Lowering your head during the downswing ■ Uncocking wrists too early on downswing ■ Shifting weight to left foot on backswing	■ Keep knees flexed at con-stant angle throughout the swing. ■ Delay wrist release as long as possible. Keep hands ahead of the ball. ■ Begin backswing with hands, arms, and shoulders as a unit.
Topping ball	■ Losing arm extension during the swing ■ Lifting head during the swing ■ Too much right arm pressure on downswing ■ Swaying forward on down-swing	■ Keep head down and still. ■ Lead downswing with legs and left side of body. ■ Swing arc should rotate around the head. ■ Anchor heel of front foot during the backswing.

on these problems, however, be sure to work on the common golf swing problems that all golfers face, such as failing to maintain the center of rotation and not initiating your backswing with your hands, arms, and shoulders as a unit. Relax; try to make your swing as relaxed and smooth as possible. Once you've addressed these problems, move on to the others.

Slicing

Far more beginning golfers slice the ball than hook it. The **slice** is caused by hitting the ball with a club face that is open relative to the swing path, which puts a clockwise spin on it (Figure 3-20). The spin causes the ball to go from left to right along a path like a banana and greatly affects the distance you get. Proper coordina-

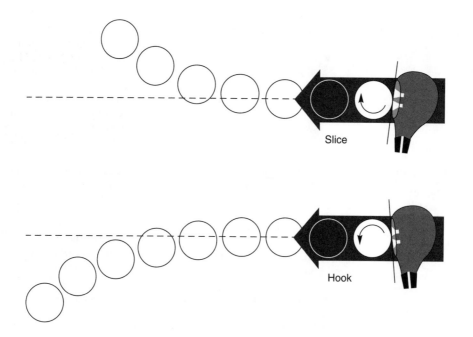

Figure 3-20

The slice and the hook. Hitting across the ball with an open (slice) or closed (hook) club face will impart spin on the ball that will change its direction of flight in the air (like a curve ball in baseball).

tion of the lower and upper body during the forward swing will help you properly align the club to the ball at impact.

Try to keep the arc of your swing consistent. As you swing through the ball, be sure the shaft, club face, and front arm are in the same positions as when you first addressed the ball at the beginning of the swing. Keep the same radius on the forward swing that you had on the backswing (radius refers to the distance between your shoulders and the end of the lever formed by your arms and club). You can do this if you don't lead with your hands during the backswing and if you initiate the forward swing with the lower body.

Moving the head to the right can cause you to slice the ball. Remember to keep your head still (and behind the ball) by making it the center of the swing arc. This, of course, is much more difficult than it sounds because keeping the head still requires good body mechanics throughout the swing in the legs and upper body.

Stance and grip can cause slicing as well. In the grip, if the V's are outside the shoulder, you may tend to slice the ball. A too-open stance can cause a slice, too. Typically, this latter may occur if you move the left foot backward during the swing. Finally, slicing can be caused by overly stiff club shafts or grips that are too large (opposite for hooking).

Bending the left elbow is another common problem with beginning golfers (Figure 3-21). This problem changes the arc of the swing very unpredictably and can cause a **shank** (ball hit at an angle to the intended direction of flight), top, hook, or slice. It is almost always caused by initiating the backswing with the hands rather than with the hands, arms, and shoulders as a unit. It can also be caused by starting the forward swing with the upper body rather than with the legs.

Hooking

A **hook** is a shot in which the flight of the ball curves from right to left (Figure 3-20). It is more common among good golfers than among beginners. It is caused by closing the club face on impact. Moving the head to the left can cause some people to hook the ball. Again, keep the head still.

Grip can also be a problem. People who use a strong grip and rotate the forearms well during the forward swing often close the club too much, which will cause the ball to hook. However, a strong grip can also help people who hook. If you don't rotate your

Figure 3-21

Don't bend the left elbow during the swing. This problem is often caused by starting the backswing with the hands instead of the hands, arms, and shoulders as a unit.

forearms enough, using a strong grip increases the possible range of motion in the arms and will straighten out the ball.

A poor swing arc can also cause a hook. Moving the arc from inside to outside with a closed club face results in a hook. This is usually caused by initiating the forward swing with the hands, which causes the in-to-out swing pattern.

Hitting Behind the Ball (Hitting the Ball Fat)

Hitting behind the ball is sometimes called **hitting the ball fat.** This occurs when a player hits the ground before making contact with the ball—and it very definitely affects power. The major cause of hitting the ball fat is initiating the forward swing with the right hand. Remember that the forward swing should begin with a forward movement of the hips, followed almost immediately by the legs, arms, and shoulders moving together. Resist the temptation to overuse the right hand.

Uncocking the wrists too early during the forward swing will also cause a player to hit the ground behind the ball. Remember, you want to be in the same position at impact as you were when you first addressed the ball.

Beginning golfers sometimes shift their weight to the left foot during the backswing, which is just the opposite of what you want to do. This shift occurs when you try to initiate and control the swing with the upper body, particularly the hands. If you turn the hands, arms, and shoulders as a unit, proper weight shift will occur naturally.

Topping the Ball

A common dread of all golfers is to be on the first tee with everyone watching and to top the ball, dribbling it on the ground 40 yards. Yet, this is a common problem for beginning golfers. It occurs for some of the same reasons that are mentioned again and again: moving outside the center of rotation, initiating the forward swing with the arms, and not swinging through the ball on the forward swing.

The most common cause of topping the ball, however, is losing arm extension during the swing. This occurs when hand movement is emphasized rather than coordination of the movement of the legs, shoulders, arms, and hands. You must swing through the ball. Again, think of the ball as simply being in the way of the swing rather than as something you swing at. Related to this is gripping the club too tightly, which encourages tightness in the arms and shoulders and causes you to "shorten" your arms.

Lifting the head during the swing is another cause of topping. You may lift your head prematurely because you want to watch your shot or you may be extending at the knees excessively during impact, which causes you to rise up during the swing. Lifting the torso or extending the knees during the swing will also cause you to top the ball.

Using too much rear arm pressure during the forward swing in an effort to increase power with the upper body can cause topping, as well. Instead, bring the arms and shoulders around as a unit and don't try so hard.

Swaying forward on the forward swing is another cause of topping. A swaying motion is usually established by lifting the heel of the front foot during the backswing. Although a small amount of heel lift is OK, leave the heel anchored if you sway during the swing. Sway makes it difficult to establish a constant swing radius. It complicates the swing—and the basic rule of consistent golf is "Keep it simple."

When trying to perfect your swing, remember that you are dealing with a complex movement with many elements. Over-emphasizing small elements of the swing will cause the movement to become mechanical. Work on only one problem at a time and integrate your changes into a total fluid swing.

Worksheet

1. Do your fingers or palms control the club during the swing? _____

2. What are the basic elements of a good golf grip?

   Top hand: _____

   _____

   _____

   Bottom hand: _____

   _____

   _____

3. What are the elements of a good golf stance? _____

   _____

   _____

4. In a _____ stance, the toes of your feet align with each other.

5. In a _____ stance, the front foot is closer to the target line than the back foot.

6. As you use shorter irons, move the ball _____ slightly,
   _____ your stance, and move your feet _____ slightly.

7. The _____ stance is better for shorter irons because it makes
   the swing arc more outward and upward.

8. In _____ alignment you can draw a line between your toes or hips or shoulders
   that's parallel to the target line.

9. Your swing should revolve around the center of your _____.

10. You should feel like your _____ is absolutely stationary during the swing movement.

11. What is an important cause of moving outside the center of rotation? _____

    _____

12. In the backswing, move your hands and arms _____ and _____
    backward as you turn your shoulders.

13.   In the backswing, the movement of the _____, _____, and _____
      occur as a single, coordinated movement.

14.   A good backswing allows for: _____
      _____

15.   At the end of the backswing, the back of the right shoulder should be _____.
      _____

16.   What are two techniques for breaking the wrists during the backswing? _____
      _____

17.   The swing should follow a continuous _____, much like the hub of a wheel.

18.   Begin the forward swing with a movement from the _____, followed
      almost immediately by the legs, arms, and shoulders moving together.

19.   During the forward swing, try to _____ you followed during the backswing.

20.   For right-handed golfers, the _____ side of the body dominates the forward swing.

21.   During the forward swing, the _____ arm remains straight and the _____ stays still.

22.   During the forward swing, return the left arm, club shaft, and club face to the same position as
      when you _____ the ball.

23.   In the follow-through, your hands should be higher than your _____ and your
      weight should be on your _____ foot, with your hips squared to the _____.

24.   In a _____ the ball travels from left to right.

25.   In a _____ the ball travels from right to left.

26.   Hitting the ball fat means that you have _____.

27.   What is the most common cause of topping the ball? _____
      _____

Shots from the Tee and Fairway

The elements of the golf swing are almost the same whether from the tee or the fairway. Stance and placement of the ball vary slightly depending on the length of the club. With a driver, the hips are more closed (toes parallel), and the ball is placed about the level of the left heel. As the club length shortens, the stance opens (toes of front foot drop behind those of the back foot), the feet are placed closer together, and the ball is moved back slightly.

A basic challenge in golf, whether hitting from the tee or the fairway, is choosing the proper club. Develop a feel for how far you can hit a ball with each club. Clubs are designed with different degrees of loft although the swing remains the same regardless of club. Choose the correct club for the distance you want to hit. If a shot looks as though it would be difficult to make with an 8-iron, drop to a 7-iron and take a normal swing—don't attempt to hit the 8-iron extra hard.

SHOTS FROM THE TEE

Tee shots are made from within the teeing ground. This is an imaginary rectangle between two tee markers that extends two club lengths from front to back. A variety of objects, such as blocks of wood or metal balls shaped like large golf balls, may be used as markers. The ball may be placed anywhere within this rectangle (the golfer may stand outside).

The choice of club from the tee depends on the distance to the hole, the width of the fairway, wind conditions, and your skill. The goal of the tee shot is to put the ball in the most advantageous position for the next shot. In a wide open fairway on a par-5 hole, a long drive is an advantage. Here, you would usually choose a driver—provided you can hit a driver with reasonable accuracy. On a narrow fairway, however, with trees and brush along the sides, you may be risking disaster trying to hit a driver as far as you can. In this case it would be better to use a 3- or 5-wood or an iron and hit an accurate shot. Don't break out the driver just because it's a long way to the hole. Professional golfers playing on a difficult course with narrow fairways not uncommonly use drivers on only three or four holes.

Of critical importance is deciding where to hit your tee shot. Play the percentages. Try to hit the ball where you are least likely to get into trouble. This means giving yourself a margin of error to avoid out of bounds and hazards. Consider the lie of the ball. It is easier to hit a ball from level ground on a part of the fairway with good access to the green than to hit from a side-hill lie or patch of bare ground. A long drive that puts you into a bad position for your next shot is often less helpful than a shot that goes a shorter distance but has a good lie.

For beginners, it is best to tee up on the same side as a potential trouble spot. For example, if a lake is on the left side of the fairway, tee up on that side of the tee box. Conversely, if potential trouble is on the right side of the fairway, tee up on the right side and aim your drive to the left. This teeing strategy gives you the widest angle for making a successful shot and avoiding potential obstacles.

Take a normal swing even when faced with hazards on the course. If the fairway has a water hazard on one side and woods on the other, don't shorten your swing in an attempt to place the ball in the middle. You are far better off using a club you feel comfortable with and taking a normal swing.

Height of the Tee

The height of the tee (the device that holds the ball; usually made of wood) varies with the club you're using. A good rule of thumb when using woods is to tee the ball so that half the ball is above the clubhead at address. As discussed, the driver should contact the ball during the ascending part of the arc, so the ball should be teed fairly high. This decreases the tendency to hit the club on the ground, which makes it easier to align the clubhead properly with the ball. With the driver, you want to sweep the ball rather than hit down at it. A slightly higher tee height allows you to accomplish this.

When you use a 3-, 4-, or 5-wood or iron, you want to tee the ball low so you contact it during the descending or flat portion of the swing. To hit irons from the teeing ground, most players tee the ball so it is barely off the ground. It is often helpful to use split tees (tees broken in half by other golfers) that you find lying around the teeing ground. These are easy to put into the ground, and they keep the ball at exactly the right height.

The Effects of Wind

Wind can obviously be a problem because it affects the flight of the ball, but it also can affect you, the heat loss from your body making you stiff and inflexible. Wind causes anxiety and disturbs concentration in golfers. You may find yourself saying, "The wind is blowing against me. I'm going to have to hit the ball hard to get it on the green." Typically, this leads to your changing your swing and hitting a less than ideal shot.

Choose the proper club for the conditions. If a 5-iron is usually appropriate for a hole, but there is a strong tail wind, a 6- or 7-iron may be better. If you are facing a strong head wind, a 4- or 3-iron may be better. A good rule of thumb is to use a club one number lower (for example, a 4-iron instead of a 5-iron) for every 10 miles an hour of wind velocity, when the wind is in your face. Whatever the conditions, however, don't change your swing— swing the club the same way!

Because wind can make your muscles tight, be sure to wear a jacket or sweater to keep your muscles warm when conditions warrant. Do warm-up exercises before you swing so you are as loose and relaxed as possible. Excessive tightness decreases the distance of your shots and interferes with proper technique.

SHOTS FROM THE FAIRWAY

Fairway shots are as important as tee shots. Golfers typically practice driving and putting more than they practice fairway iron shots. Yet, you always face these shots during a round of golf. In fact, you face more of them than drives in a typical round, so it makes sense to practice them.

Fairway conditions vary much more than conditions on the tee or putting green. You face irregular lies, obstructions, hazards, and optical illusions. Fairway shots include those made with woods and irons, hazard shots, pitches, and chips.

Fairway Woods

Use fairway woods when you want to hit the ball a great distance. The 3-, 4-, and 5-woods are those most commonly used from the fairway. With these clubs, you hit the ball during the flat portion of the bottom of the swing arc. Be sure to do so without hitting the ground. As discussed, hitting the ground first deflects the clubhead and causes a deviation from the ideal swing arc.

The 5-wood has become particularly popular with golfers. It is the easiest of the woods to handle, puts a high loft on the ball, and moves more easily through the grass in the rough because of its small head size. The higher loft imparted on the ball is some-times an advantage because the ball doesn't roll as far after it hits the ground. A ball hit with a 5-wood that lands on the green has minimal roll and stops sooner than a shot made with a 3-wood. Some senior women's players have had great success with a 7-wood, which they find easier to use than a 5-wood.

When hitting a fairway wood (3, 4, and 5), align yourself so the ball is further behind your left heel than it is when you use the driver. This position helps align the club face with the ball so you can lift the ball into the air more easily. You can ensure proper loft from your fairway woods if you hit through the ball and finish high on your follow-through. Avoid chopping at the ball, particularly if you have a less than ideal lie. Chopping fairway wood shots often shank (move the ball at an abrupt angle) to one side or the other.

Fairway Irons

The technique for hitting the 1–9 irons from the fairway is essen-tially the same as for other clubs. Most beginning golfers, and even professionals, avoid the 1- and 2-irons because of their length and smaller sweet spots (place on club head where the weight is cen-tered). The development of cavity-back 1- and 2-irons (see Chap-ter 2) has made these long irons easier to hit, but they still cause problems for most golfers.

Determine your choice of iron on the fairway by the distance you want to hit the ball. Figure 2-1 in Chapter 2 shows the distance that an average golfer hits the ball with the various irons. The distance you hit the ball with a particular iron may vary from the average. Develop a feel for your capacity and typical performance with each club—and, of course, no matter which club you choose, take the same swing every time. In general, keep the tempo the same on every shot; use the same swing speed for long irons as for short irons; and take a relaxed swing using good fundamentals.

Because of the length of the clubs and loft of the club face, you should take a slightly narrower stance as you progress from long to shorter irons (Figure 4-1). With all irons, hit the ball on the downward path. This imparts backspin on the ball that helps lift it into the air (Figure 4-2). Backspin occurs when the ball rides up

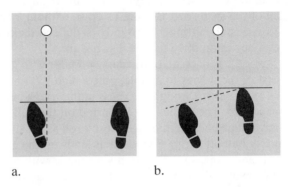

a.   b.

Figure 4-1

The stance for a driver and midlength iron (4-iron). (a) For the driver, the stance is square and the ball is aligned with the front heel. (b) When hitting irons, address the ball further behind the left heel than you do with the driver. This helps you make contact with the ball during the downward portion of the swing arc.

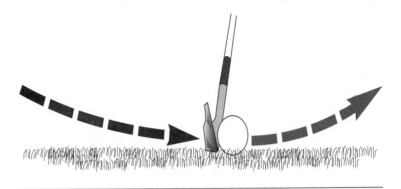

Figure 4-2

Make contact with the ball before hitting the ground. This puts backspin on the ball that helps lift it into the air.

the face of the club. The clubhead should contact the ball before hitting the ground so you can control the direction of the swing arc.

Alignment is particularly critical in making successful shots from the fairway. As with shots from the tee, position yourself in a line parallel to the line between the ball and the target. As noted in Chapter 3, a good technique to ensure proper alignment is to aim at a point, such as a clump of grass, divot, or tee, that is aligned at an intermediate distance between the ball and the target.

Irregular Lies   One of the major challenges of playing shots from the fairway is hitting from **irregular lies**—that is, hitting balls from a surface that is slanted uphill, downhill, or sideways. Slanted surfaces throw off the relationships among the body's joints. Balance is usually disturbed and weight is abnormally transferred to one leg or the other.

Downhill Lies   Maintaining good balance is very important with downhill lies. Good balance helps you hit the ball into the air and prevents you from hitting the ball fat (hitting the ground before hitting the ball). Good balance also helps prevent the normal tendency to hit the ball to the right when faced with this type of lie (because your weight tends to be centered more on your front foot than normal).

Although you want to maintain your normal swing as much as possible when hitting any kind of irregular lie, there are several changes you need to make to hit the ball off the ground with accuracy. Align your shoulders with the slope of the fairway and put more of your weight on your left leg than normal (Figure 4-3). The natural tendency to lean left during the swing is good because it aligns you better with the slope of the fairway.

Also, try to slow your swing so you can maintain balance. Keep your swing mechanics the same—just try to be smoother and more deliberate. Be particularly careful about keeping your head still. It is easy to slide past the ball because of the effects of gravity. To prevent the ball from going to the right, aim the shot a little to the left.

Align yourself so the ball is back more than usual. Hit the ball into the air by making sure the clubhead is running parallel to the slope at impact. Your choice of club will dictate the amount of loft. An iron typically lofts the ball less on a downhill lie than it does on level ground, so you must choose a shorter club than normal. For example, if a shot would normally call for a 7-iron, use an 8-iron instead and you will probably get the same degree of loft.

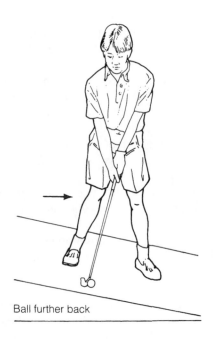

Ball further back

Figure 4-3

Playing the downhill lie. Position your body so the ball is further back. Lean with the slope—the body should set up at the same angle as the ground.

Uphill Lies   Some of the same principles that apply for downhill lies apply to uphill lies as well. Again, align yourself with the slope of the hill (Figure 4-4). Play the ball forward in your stance. When hitting uphill, place more weight on your back foot. If you lean on the uphill foot, you will drive the ball downward. During the backswing, keep your front foot firmly anchored to the ground to prevent swaying backward. You may have to flex your left leg more than usual to improve balance. During the forward swing, keep your weight back on your right foot to aid balance. More your left arm vigorously toward the ball to compensate for gravity pushing you down the hill. Your swing depends much more on the action of the hands and arms than it does when hitting from the level.

When hitting uphill, the ball acts differently from the way it acts when hitting downhill. The ball lofts higher and has a tendency to move to the left. To compensate for these effects, aim a little to the right and choose a longer club. Keep the ball in the

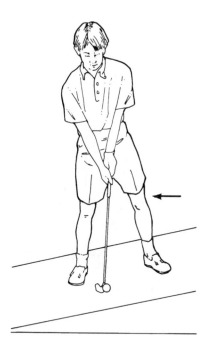

Figure 4-4

Playing the uphill lie. Put more weight on the back foot—let the body tilt with the angle of the land.

same relative position as on level ground unless the slope of the fairway is severe. In that case, move the ball closer to your front foot.

   Side-hill Lies   Shots from side-hill lies can severely alter your swing. The most important principle for hitting a side-hill lie is to adjust the flex in your legs so you have better alignment with the ball.

   If the ball is above your feet (Figure 4-5a) adjust the lie of the club by choking up on the grip. Your arms should hang naturally so you can make as close to a normal shot as possible. Put your weight on the balls of your feet to counteract the tendency to fall away from the ball. Use a longer than normal club so you have a near normal swing arc. A fairway wood is sometimes a good club for this type of side-hill lie because it is longer and the clubhead is curved.

   If the ball is below your feet, hold the club at the end of the grip (Figure 4-5b). The problem with this shot is that you tend to

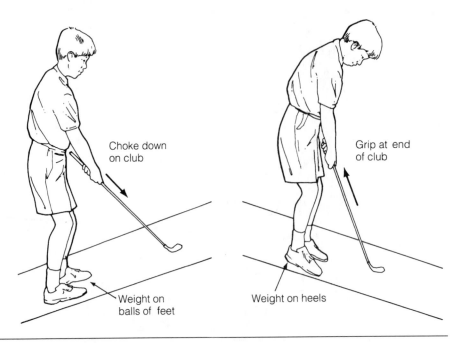

Choke down
on club

Grip at end
of club

Weight on
balls of feet

Weight on heels

Figure 4-5
Playing side-hill lies. Adjust the knee flex to help you get level with the ball.

lean over during the address. Go to a stronger club (lower number) so you can swing from a more erect posture. For example, if a shot normally calls for a 7-iron, use a 6-iron and swing a little easier.

The ball will follow the contour of the slope after you hit it. Like other irregular lies, side-hill lies tend to veer to the side. You will tend to hit balls with downward side-hill lies to the right and balls with upward side-hill lies to the left. Compensate for these tendencies by aligning yourself slightly to the other side.

Avoiding Obstacles   Having a tree between the ball and the green or your target is not uncommon—and there is no one way to play such a shot. You may choose to hit the ball low under the branches or hit it high, over the tree. Your course of action depends entirely on your distance from the tree and distance to the hole.

If you are close to the tree and decide to go low, choose a longer club that doesn't loft the ball as much. If the hole is close, you have to slow your swing to avoid overhitting the ball. Or you may use a shorter iron, moving the ball back in your stance, and breaking the wrists earlier during the swing. This has the effect of closing the club face when you contact the ball. As you can see, both techniques require a lot of finesse.

If you are far enough from the tree, you may consider a high shot. Again, your choice of clubs depends on the distance to the hole. If you are close, then a pitching wedge is probably most appropriate. If you are a long way from the pin, a long iron can effectively give you more loft. Align the ball slightly forward in your stance, holding the club a the end of the grip. Hit through the ball with a lively wrist action and with a full swing so you give it backspin and loft it upward. The hands should be about even with the club head when you hit the ball.

As you will learn in Chapter 8, when faced with trouble on the course (for example, when your ball is lying behind a tree in the rough), avoid hitting low percentage shots. Although you may score a winner and save the hole by trying a desperation shot over the tree, it is more likely that you will hit the tree and perhaps lose the ball—leaving you in the same spot where you started but with a stroke added to your score. Sometimes it is better to accept a loss, hitting the ball into a playable position on the fairway, rather than risk losing many strokes because of a low percentage gamble.

Hitting from Divots   Although you can move a ball from its own ball mark if it becomes imbedded, you cannot move a ball if it comes to rest in another golfer's **divot** (see Chapter 6). The secret to overcoming this difficult lie is to hit down and through the ball, making contact with it before you hit the ground. Stand with the ball slightly behind the point you normally play it so you catch it during the downward portion of the swing arc. Actively move your hips and arms to contact the ball as early as possible during the downswing.

You should almost never use a wood from a divot because of the difficulty in getting under the ball. After you have been in this situation a few times, you are much more aware of the importance of repairing any divots you make on the course.

Hitting from Bare, Hard Ground   Many courses have patches of bare ground or roads that are not out of bounds. Often local variations of the rules allow you to move your ball. Information about local rules appears on the back of the scorecard (see

Chapter 6). However, at other times, you need to play the ball as it lies.

The secret to making this shot successfully is to not hit the ground before striking the ball. If you do, your clubhead will bounce easily off the hard ground and you will likely top the ball. The strategy for hitting shots from these locations is similar to that for hitting shots from divots: Stand with the ball slightly back and hit down on the ball. Try to "pick it clean." As with divots, woods are not recommended when making shots from bare ground because of the difficulty in getting under the ball.

HITTING FROM BUNKERS

Beginning golfers often cringe when they land in a sand bunker on the fairway or close to the hole. This is understandable because the ball may be partially inbedded in the sand, the golfer is forbidden from grounding the club (touching the sand with the club at address), and balance is difficult. The number one goal for all sand shots is to get the ball out of the trap. If the ball is in a fairway bunker 200 yards from the green but you are buried in the sand next to the lip of the trap, use a sand wedge to get back on the fairway. If you use a wood, you will likely hit the lip and the ball will remain in the trap. It is better to lose a stroke playing it safe than to waste two or three strokes trying to hit a life-saving miracle shot from the bunker.

Fairway Bunkers

Landing in a fairway bunker need not be a total disaster, provided the ball isn't buried in the sand or you are not too close to the lip of the trap. Because bunkers usually lie along the sides of a fairway and are long and flat, balls tend to roll into them and not become imbedded the way they do in bunkers close to the green. If you are fortunate, you can play the bunker shot like an ordinary shot from the fairway. If your ball has landed on a clump of grass within the trap, it is even permissible to ground the club.

Beginners should usually use a 4- or 5-iron from fairway bunkers. These clubs help you get a good "bite" on the ball. Dig your feet into the sand so your position is well-balanced and secure. Spread your feet apart slightly more than you would during a comparable fairway shot. You are forbidden to ground your club in a hazard. Grip up on the club to compensate for the club length you have lost. Address the ball between your feet and attempt to hit it

Figure 4-6

Hitting the ball from a fairway bunker. Address the ball between your feet and try to hit it squarely, making little or no contact with the sand. "Pick" the ball from the sand.

squarely, making little or no contact with the sand (Figure 4-6). *Note:* you can hit the sand with the club during the stroke but not at address. Although you want to hit the ball first, you want to contact it during the bottom of the forward swing so you can have a clean follow-through. Try to swing level and "pick" the ball clean from the bunker. It is very difficult to get your legs into the shot the way you can on the fairway because your feet are buried in the sand, but try to relax, keep your head still, and take a smooth and easy shot.

Green-Side Bunkers

In green-side bunker shots, you make little or no contact with the ball. Instead, you contact the sand behind the ball, and the ball moves due to displacement of the sand below it. The ideal club for these shots is a sand wedge, a club that has a large flange on the bottom that prevents excessive penetration into the sand. If you don't have a sand wedge, a pitching wedge or 9-iron will do very well.

Dig your feet into the sand as described for shots from fairway bunkers. Use a slightly open stance and place a little more of your weight than usual on your front foot. Grip the club so the club face is more open (has a greater face angle), which provides more loft. Aim your club for the sand about 1½-4 inches behind the ball. The club should progress behind, under, and through the ball (Figure 4-7, Figure 4-8). When contacting the ball, accelerate through it—deceleration will cause the ball to remain in the sand. Keep the movement of the swing slow because this allows the club to penetrate the sand more easily. Because of a more abrupt angle of arm swing, you will have increased wrist action at the bottom of the swing arc. The arm and body positions are more like a V than a y because your stance is narrower and your arm swing is active but with little trunk rotation. Although the length of the backswing is not as great as for shots on the fairway, follow through completely and let the left arm dominate the swing. Most of the power for this shot comes from the upper body. However, many professional golfers have active leg action that helps them give the ball more spin. As a beginner, keep the movement simple.

The distance you hit the ball out of the trap is determined by the distance behind the ball at which the club entered the sand, the angle at which the clubhead entered the sand, and the clubhead speed. If you want the ball to go further, give the club a shallower trajectory as it enters the sand and hit it closer to the ball. A deeper trajectory will make the ball leave the trap at a higher angle and consequently not go as far. You can control clubhead

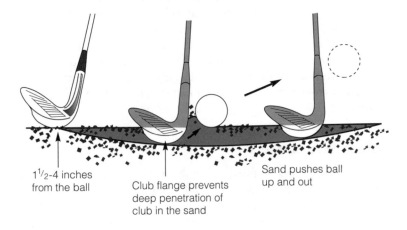

1½-4 inches
from the ball

Club flange prevents
deep penetration of
club in the sand

Sand pushes ball
up and out

Figure 4-7
Path of the clubhead when hitting a green-side bunker shot. The club should progress behind, under, and through the ball.

a. b. c. d.

Figure 4-8

Technique for hitting a ball out of a green-side sand trap. (a) Anchor feet securely and don't ground the club at address. (b) During the swing, the upper body dominates the motion. (c) Strike the sand behind the ball. (d) Follow through.

speed by regulating the speed of your arm action during the stroke. If the ball is buried, you need to hit it with a steeper trajectory. The ball will pop out of the trap with very little spin and roll when it hits the green.

THE SHORT GAME: PITCHES AND CHIPS

A **pitch** is a shot typically made less than 100 yards from the green, where the ball travels mostly through the air. The shot is usually made with a pitching wedge or sand wedge. Because the ball is lofted high in the air, it tends to stop close to where it lands. Thus, an effective pitch shot must be placed as close as possible to the hole. A pitch may be used quite close to the hole, such as when you need to hit the ball over a bunker that is directly in front of the pin.

A **chip** shot, conversely, is a low shot that hits the fairway or green and rolls for some distance. It is usually it 15 feet or less

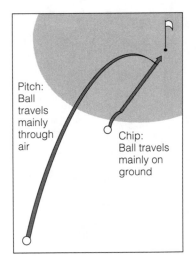

Pitch:
Ball
travels
mainly
through
air

Chip:
Ball travels
mainly on
ground

Figure 4-9

Flight path of a pitch and a chip shot. During a pitch, the ball travels mainly through the air. During a chip, the ball travels mainly on the ground.

from the green. You can chip with almost any iron, but most golfers seldom use anything longer than a 4- or 5-iron. The chip shot is used when the ball is close to the green and the golfer wants to get the ball over a short expanse of remaining fairway or green apron before having the ball roll onto the green. A comparison of a pitch and chip shot is shown in Figure 4-9.

The Pitch

Pitches are generally made with the 8- or 9-iron, pitching wedge, or sand wedge (although shots with longer clubs could technically be called pitches). Grip the club in the standard manner, but use a narrower and more open stance than you do when playing the other irons and woods. Because of the narrow, open stance, the wrists become involved sooner than during a normal swing. Distance is determined by the length of the backswing. Mastering this shot requires that you become good at estimating how far back to swing the club. A common mistake is taking a backswing that is too short and then trying to compensate by punching the ball during the downswing. Another common mistake is to take a normal full backswing, then attempt to decelerate the club so you don't hit the ball too far. Both mistakes lead to inconsistency and errant shots.

Control is very important during the pitch. Some players find that choking down on the club by 1 to 2 inches increases their control and touch. As with most other shots, try to hit through the ball and follow-through fully. An example of a pitch shot at a medium distance is shown in Figure 4-10.

It takes a long time to master pitches, but doing so is critical to success in golf. When you practice, stress accuracy and try to place the ball next to a target from varying distances. Work on swinging deliberately, and experiment with different size backswings so you develop a better feel for distance when you play on the course.

The Chip Shot

As discussed, use a chip shot when the ball is close to the green and you want to get over a short distance of grass covering the last portion of fairway or green apron before reaching the green. You can use almost any iron, but the most popular is the 7-iron. Use a longer iron when the ball is further from the pin and you want the ball to have little backspin. The shorter clubs will cause the ball to spin and grip the green as it hits, thus preventing it from running

a.   b.   c.

d.   e.

Figure 4-10

A pitch shot, medium distance. (a) Use an open stance with feet
relatively close together. (b) Distance is determined by the length
of the backswing. (c) Take the club back smoothly without picking
it up with the hands. (d) Hit through the ball and (e) follow
through fully.

too much. However, too much spin can lead to balls that fall short
of the target.

A chip shot is shown in Figure 4-11. You can use almost any
grip for a chip shot. Although many golfers use a standard overlapping, or Vardon, grip (see Chapter 3), others use special putting grips (see Chapter 5). The grip should be firm but not tight
during the shot. Assume a narrow, open stance, with shoulders
parallel and the ball aligned slightly back of center of the body's

Figure 4-11

Elements of the chip shot: narrow, open stance; ball behind midline; weight over front foot. Use a pendulum-type stroke. The wrist should remain firm and the hands should stay ahead of the ball.

midline. Weight should be centered over the front foot. Grip down on the club for better control. Align your head so it is over the ball. Use a pendulum-type stroke in which you move away from the ball during the backswing and forward through the ball during the forward swing. The swing should be shallow and its arc should resemble a shallow saucer. The wrist should remain firm during the stroke, and the hands should stay ahead of the ball during the entire movement. Keep your right hand (left for left-handed players) under the left. The movement is like throwing a ball underhand.

For most golfers, chipping is much less precise a movement than putting. Thus, if you are near the green or on the apron of the green and the grass is not too thick, you can putt the ball.

Worksheet

1.   As the club length shortens, the stance _____, the feet are placed _____

_____ and the ball is moved _____.

2.   When faced with potential trouble on a hole, such as a water hazard, where is it best to tee up?

_____

3.   When using a driver on the teeing ground, tee the ball so that half the ball is above _____

_____ at address.

4.   In what part of the swing arc do you make contact with the ball when using fairway woods?

_____

5.   When hitting a fairway wood (3, 4, and 5), align yourself so the ball is _____

your left heel than when using the driver.

6.   What basic principle should you keep in mind when playing the ball on a slope? _____

_____

7.   What basic principle should you keep in mind when playing the ball from bare, hard ground?

_____

8.   When hitting the ball from a bunker, it is forbidden to _____.

9.   Describe contact when hitting the ball from a green-side bunker. _____

_____

10.   A pitch is a shot, typically made less than 100 yards from the green, where the ball travels

_____.

11.   In a chip shot, the ball travels mainly _____.

5

Putting

"You drive for show, but you putt for dough!" Although this famous golf saying is an overstatement, there is a lot of truth to it. At one time or another, all golfers have hit a great shot from the tee and succeeded by a masterful approach shot to land 25 feet from the pin—only to 3- or 4-putt the green. To be a good golfer, you must be able to put long putts to within 4 to 6 feet of the hole and sink short putts consistently. If you can't, you will never be a good golfer no matter how good your shots from the tee or fairway.

Fifty percent of allotted strokes in golf are putts. If you practice enough and have reasonably good technique, you can become a good putter. You may not have the power or skill to hit like a Nick Faldo or Nancy Lopez, but you can become as good as they are on the putting green. If you can cut down on the number of putts you make on the green by one stroke on every other hole, you have made a large improvement in your golf game. An improvement like this is simply a matter of practice and developing sound fundamentals.

As with shots you make with woods and irons, putting requires consistent technique to be successful. The distance and lie of the putt demand some variation, but, in general, you should try to stroke the ball exactly the same way every time you putt.

Unlike strokes with irons and woods, there is no universally recognized way to putt. If you watch professionals, you will see a wide variety of styles ranging from the knocked-kneed technique of Arnold Palmer to the modified upright straddle technique (the golfer is upright and uses a long putter) made popular by Sam Snead. However, although styles differ, the mechanics of the stroke vary little. Certain basic principles are common to any successful putting technique. Begin with a conventional pendulum putting method and modify it if necessary as you start to develop "touch" on the green (touch is the capacity to stroke the ball with just the right amount of force to sink the putt).

THE GRIP

There are many ways to grip a golf club while putting. The most common methods are the overlapping, reverse overlapping, and opposing grips (Figure 5-1). The overlapping grip is almost the same one used for tee and fairway shots except that you hold your hands so they are more opposite each other as you grip the club. As before, the little finger of the right hand overlaps the forefinger

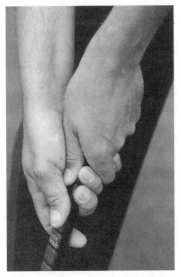 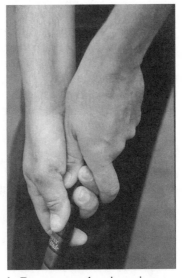 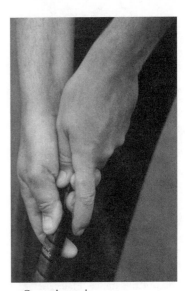

a. Overlapping (or Vardon) grip   b. Reverse overlapping grip   c. Opposing grip

Figure 5-1
Common putting grips.

of the left hand. (Again, descriptions here are for right-handed players; for left-handed players, reverse these.)

The **reverse overlapping grip** is a slight variation of the overlapping grip. Here, the index finger of the left hand (top hand) overlaps the ring finger of the right hand. All fingers of the dominant hand are in contact with the club, which helps give greater control.

In the **opposing grip,** cradle the club between the right and left hands, almost as though you were praying. The hands are opposite each other, on the sides of the club shaft. This grip is excellent for performing a pendulum motion, a putting style popular with many golfers.

THE STANCE

Take a comfortable stance with feet about 12 inches apart. Distribute your weight evenly between toes and heels, and between left and right feet (Figure 5-2). If you prefer to put more weight on one foot, choose the back foot because this will help you stay behind the ball and give you a slightly better perspective on the line between the ball and the hole. Some experts suggest putting the weight over the left foot because this position is better for keeping the head over the ball. In putting, individual preference, almost more than anything else, dictates the correct technique.

Bend at the knees and waist and let your arms extend naturally. You may find that you have better stability if you let your knees bow inward in a slightly knock-kneed position. Try to keep your elbows close to the body to decrease variability in your shots.

Your line of sight should be over and slightly to the rear of the ball, which is positioned at or slightly behind your left foot. Align the putter (on contact with the ball), your stance, and your line of sight parallel to the hole. If you turn your head in an unusual way, its position may create optical illusions that will make it difficult to putt well consistently. As you check your alignment to the hole, twist your head to the left without moving the rest of your body. If you raise out of your stance to sight the hole, you will find it difficult to align yourself again.

Figure 5-2

The putting stance: Place feet about 12 inches apart and distribute your weight evenly. Bend at the knees and waist and let your arms extend naturally. Line up so your line of sight is over and slightly to the rear of the ball.

THE PUTTING STROKE

The putting stroke uses both arms in a motion that resembles a pendulum (Figure 5-3). The left hand and arm do most of the active work, while the right hand stabilizes the stroke. Fix the left

a.   b.   c.

Figure 5-3

The putting stroke. Use both arms in a motion that resembles a pendulum. (a) The left hand and arm are active, while the right hand stabilizes the stroke. (b) The club face meets the ball squarely on impact. (c) Continue to move forward during the follow-through. Make your backswing and your follow-through the same length.

wrist during the forward part of the stroke. The left arm should continue to move forward during the follow-through. This provides a smooth, level stroking action on the ball at impact. If the left arm stops at impact, the stroke will be jerky and have an unpredictable and inconsistent effect on the path of the ball.

The path of the club face is not straight up and back during the swing. With a pendulum swing, the club face always stays square to the arc, meeting the ball squarely on impact. Try to contact the ball on the center of the club face—the sweet spot. If you hit the ball too close to the heel or toe of the club face, you will likely hit it at an angle. You also may put spin on the ball that will change its course on the putting green. Putter head acceleration—keeping the putter moving aggressively during the stroke—is important for keeping the stroke and putter square to the target during contact. Try to make your backswing and your follow-through the same length.

As with tee and fairway shots, hit through the ball rather than striking at it. The forward and backward swing should be as smooth as possible. The length of the backswing should be proportional to the distance of the putt. Try not to change speeds abruptly during the swing because this adds inconsistency to the motion. Maintain a constant grip pressure throughout the putt.

As with strokes from the tee and fairway, keep your head still. Avoid the temptation to lift your head as you strike the ball. Be careful not to let your body or head sway during the putting movement. Get set before the putt. Although it is important for you to keep your head down when you putt, you also need to "read" the slope of the green (that is, judge the green's slope and speed). After you make contact with the ball, look up and follow the ball's path, particularly if and when it passes the hole. The movement of the ball will give you clues about where to aim the comeback putt.

STRATEGIES FOR SUCCESSFUL PUTTING

The allotted number of strokes on the putting green is two. If you can consistently sink your putts in two to three strokes per hole and occasionally sink them in one stroke, you are doing well. As discussed, putting makes up a large part of the game. You have to practice to develop touch and consistency. Work on your putting as much as you do the rest of your game. You can even practice on the living room rug in your home. Put a dime down and aim at it—when you get to the course the cup will seem huge.

Long Putts

Making 30- to 40-foot putts with any consistency is difficult. When you consider factors such as green contours, grass length and growing angle, degree of wetness, and other irregularities in the playing surface, you can see why. Rather than trying for the hole every time on a long putt, try to put the ball within 6 feet of it (Figure 5-4). This gives you an area 12 feet in diameter on either side of the hole at which to aim. It's much easier to put a ball within an area like this than directly into a hole that's only 4¼ inches wide.

Spot putting can sometimes help you achieve a good line for a long putt. Pick a spot directly on the line between the hole and your ball. The spot may be a discoloration in the green surface or a thin spot in the grass. Putt through your chosen spot on the way to

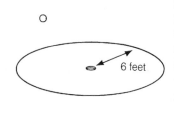

Figure 5-4

When putting long, try to put the ball within 6 feet of the hole.

the hole. This technique is helpful because it is easier to putt accurately toward a closer object than to one that is further away.

Short Putts

Hit the ball firmly on short putts and aim for the back of the cup. The only exception to this is a severely down-sloped short putt. Here you must finesse the ball into the hole with a light tap. For most short putts, maintain a fluid putting stroke, just as you do for longer putts. Follow through and make your backward and forward strokes equidistant; for example, if your back stroke is 5 inches, make sure your follow-through also goes 5 inches. When putting less than 6 feet, aim at a point within the hole (unless there is a severe break). On short putts, it is particularly important to keep your head down during the stroke. Avoid the temptation to lift your head prematurely.

Practice short putts until you can sink them a high percentage of the time. Go to the putting green and practice 1-foot putts. Set a standard for yourself. For example, practice at that distance until you can sink 19 out of 20. When you reach your goal, practice at a slightly greater distance—for instance, at 1½ to 2 feet—and repeat the procedure. Practice level, side-hill, downhill, and uphill putts at these distances so that you will feel confident when you encounter them playing golf. Above all, develop a sense of confidence on the practice green.

Be Decisive When You Putt

An old saying about putting is "Never up, never in." Good putters tend to putt the ball beyond the hole; poor putters tend to be short. A good strategy is to hit the ball so it goes 12 inches past the hole if it isn't on the mark. Putt through the hole. Hitting the ball firmly tends to make it go straighter. In general, if you have to putt uphill, aim for the back of the hole. If you have a downhill lie, aim for the front edge of the hole. When putting on a green with a right to left or left to right contour, putt to the top of the hole. Of course, this advice may have to be modified slightly depending on the distance of the ball from the cup and on the slope and cut of the green. On short putts, putt straight toward the hole because the ball won't break much (*break* is side movement of the ball due to a sloping green). It's better to take a more direct route and decisively putt the ball straight into the hole.

Many people do well on longer putts but freeze up on all-important 3- to 6-foot putts. Don't think about the mechanics of the putt. Rather, relax and think positively about making it. As discussed, make shorter putts as smooth as longer ones. When you

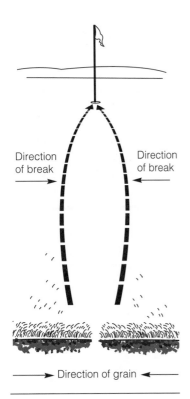

Direction of break

Direction of break

Direction of grain

Figure 5-5
Grain often determines the direction a putt will break on the green.

tense up, you change the pace of the stroke—and that leads to mistakes.

Watch the Green

Reading greens to determine breaks and the speed the ball will travel during the putt is difficult and requires a lot of practice. In this, as in other areas, experience is the best teacher. Watch your opponent's ball when he or she putts. Does the ball break to the right when it's 2 feet from the cup? Is the green fast or slow? You can tell a lot about the condition of the playing surface by watching other people putt the ball.

Watch the movement of your own shots on the green as well. If you miss a shot and go past the hole, carefully note the path of the ball. You are going to have to retrace that same ground. The grain of the grass is important in determining the speed of the putt. If you putt against the grain, the ball will travel more slowly than if you hit with the grain. If you hit across the grain, the ball will break in the direction of the growth of the grass (Figure 5-5).

Eyesight

Poor eyesight can keep you from putting well, and glasses that correct your vision for reading may not be appropriate for concentrating on a small object 4 feet away. If you have a visual deficiency, getting your eyes checked could improve your golf game.

Develop a Routine

Begin thinking about putting the ball even when you are on the tee. Observe the pin placement and the impediments you must overcome, such as bunkers, bare ground, and water hazards, to place the ball at an advantageous position on the green. Plan your fairway strategy so you take the fewest risks and have the best chance of putting the ball in the hole in one or two strokes.

Develop a preparatory routine that you follow before every putt. Study the contour and slope of the green. Look at the direction of the green. Pay attention to the water content on the surface and topsoil. And, as discussed, observe what happens to the ball when other people putt. Do these things every time and you will be more consistent on the putting green.

CARE OF THE GREEN

It is not possible or desirable to have a greens keeper on every hole to watch every player. Every golfer is responsible for helping

a.   b.   c.

Figure 5-6

The procedure for repairing ball marks on the putting green. (a, b)
Use a tee to loosen the area around the ball mark. (c) Press down
on the area with your putter to help smooth the green.

to maintain the course. Be sure to repair ball marks, small craters
made on the green when the ball hits it from the tee or fairway.
The proper procedure for repairing a ball mark is to use a tee or a
green repair tool (Figure 5-6) to gently pry up the grass around the
mark. Then press on the ball mark with the tool so the lip of the
hole is flattened against the surface of the green.

Be careful of the green when walking on it. Spikes can tear up
a green if you drag your feet. Some types of shoes, such as those
used on indoor football fields (that is, Astroturf shoes) are particularly hard on putting greens. Keep golf carts off the green. A
heavy golf cart can compact or put tire marks on delicate putting
greens and ruin the playing surface for other golfers. Care of the
course is covered further in Chapter 6 on the etiquette and rules of
golf.

Putting Etiquette

Poor etiquette on the putting green is very disturbing to many
golfers. Get in the habit of marking your ball properly and shoot-
ing only when it's your turn. Putting etiquette is discussed in
Chapter 6.

Worksheet

1. Fifty percent of allotted strokes in golf are _____.

2. What are the three most common grips for putting? _____,
    _____ and _____

3. When putting, how should you distribute your weight? _____
    _____

4. Name several principles of addressing the ball during putting. _____
    _____
    _____
    _____

5. The putting stroke uses both arms in a motion that resembles that of a _____.

6. The club face meets the ball _____ on impact.

7. The length of the backswing should be _____.

8. Why is it important to watch the movement of the ball on the green after you putt it? _____
    _____

9. The allotted number of strokes on the putting green to achieve par is _____.

Etiquette and Rules

Golf requires precision and a lot of concentration. It is little wonder, therefore, that an elaborate set of rules governing personal behavior and golf procedures have evolved. Golf etiquette helps maintain order on the golf course and helps each player concentrate fully on the game. The rules of golf help equalize the challenge of the game for all players.

ETIQUETTE

Golf etiquette includes three basic principles: (1) respect other players' concentration and well-being, (2) play briskly, and (3) help maintain the course. Golf etiquette is largely common sense and involves treating people and the course with respect.

Respect Other Players' Concentration and Well-Being

Two of the most important principles of golf etiquette involve respect. They are

- Don't do anything that might hurt someone.
- Don't disturb a player's concentration.

The first principle involves respect for the safety of other players. The second involves respect for the games of other golfers and for the sport itself. The basic principles of golf etiquette are given in Table 6-1.

Practice Safety on the Course Although golf is usually not physically perilous like football or boxing, there are potential dangers. In golf you hit small, very hard balls at high velocities using metal clubs swung at high speeds. If you hit someone with a ball or club, you can seriously injure them.

On the tee, be sure other players in your group are not in danger of being hit by a club, ball, divot, or broken clubhead. Be particularly alert when you are taking practice swings, either on or just off the tee. If you are warming up off the tee, be careful not to aim at anyone as you hit at dirt, tees, twigs, or anything else you may

---

TABLE 6-1

Important Points of Etiquette

RESPECT OTHER PLAYERS' CONCENTRATION AND WELL-BEING

- Never hit a ball until the players in front of you are out of range of your shot. On the tee, make sure other players in your group are not in danger from being hit by a club, ball, divot, or broken clubhead.
- Don't bother other players when they are making a stroke. This includes not talking, moving, or standing in their line of sight.
- Allow the player with the honor to make his or her shot before you tee up your ball.
- Shout "Fore" if a player on the course is in danger of being hit by your ball. "Fore" is also used to warn players that you are about to hit a ball in their general direction.

PLAY BRISKLY

- Complete your stroke in a timely manner.
- If you are slowing up the flow on the golf course, let other groups play through.
- Structure your play so that the game proceeds briskly.

HELP MAINTAIN THE GOLF COURSE

- Don't take more than one practice swing.
- Replace all divots and repair ball marks.
- Rake and smooth out bunkers after using them.
- Take great care not to damage the greens with improper shoes, by standing on the hole, throwing down the flag, leaning on your putter, or parking a golf cart on it.
- Don't litter.

be using as a target. Such objects can easily cause an eye injury. Also, be sure you have enough room to swing the club without striking anyone.

Be careful not to hit other players standing on the fairways or greens. When you are playing on a fairway, there is nothing more disconcerting than having someone on the tee drive a ball over your head. Never hit a ball until the players in front of you are out of range of your shot. If you hit someone from the tee, you may not only hurt the person but be held legally responsible. If you are on a par-3 hole and wish to *hit up* (hit a shot from the tee before the group on the green has begun putting), be sure the group has given you permission (usually by waving a club in the air) and has moved off the green. You can injure players putting on the green if they are unaware that you are hitting up.

Shout "fore" if a player on the course is in danger of being hit by your ball. The nature of golf makes it inevitable that other players will occasionally be in danger of being hit with a ball. If you hit a ball in the general direction of other players, you are obligated to shout "fore."

This is particularly important when you are playing a golf course with adjacent fairways that have few barriers between them. "Fore" is the correct term to use and is understood by all golfers. Don't use terms such as "Heads up" or "In-coming" be-cause your meaning may not be clear. Conversely, if you hear "fore," be alert and cover your head to protect it from possibly being hit.

Avoid Distracting Other Golfers   Distractions make it dif-ficult to concentrate and take some enjoyment out of the game.

Don't disturb other players when they are making a stroke. This includes not talking, moving, or standing in a player's line of sight (Figure 6-1). Try to stand out of range of a golfer's peripheral vision as well. This rule of etiquette applies to all players, whether on the tee, the fairway, or the green.

Allow the player with the honor to make his or her shot first. **Honor** is the privilege to play first from the teeing ground. On the first tee, this is decided by lot. After that, the honor goes to the person with the best score on the previous hole. If there was a tie score on the previous hole, the honor stays with the person who had it before. Don't make preparations for your turn at the tee until the previous player finishes.

On the fairways and greens, the person whose ball is furthest from the hole shoots first. As on the tee, stay alert to what other golfers in your group are doing and don't disturb them during their shots.

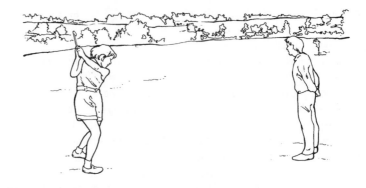

Figure 6-1
On the tee, players should stand out of the line of sight of the person hitting the ball.

Play Briskly

"Play briskly" doesn't mean that you should rush your game or run along the fairway between shots. Rather, it means that you shouldn't delay the game. These days, because of golf's popularity and the large number of players using the course at the same time, a round can easily take four or five hours. This can clearly lessen the pleasure of playing the game. Every golfer has a responsibility to keep the flow of traffic moving on the course.

Complete your stroke promptly. Decide which club you're going to use before you get to the ball so you are ready to hit when it's your turn. You can do this easily if your ball is clearly visible on the fairway and you can estimate the distance you want to hit on the next shot. When it's your turn, don't stand over the ball too long. Take a practice swing, address the ball, and hit it.

Don't take more than one practice swing. Gerry Vroom, the great golf coach from San Jose State, used to say that if a beginner takes five or six practice swings waiting for one that feels good, the chances against repeating that perfect swing are astronomical. One practice swing is permissible and serves as a light warm-up, but more than that wastes time. Save your practice for the driving range.

Don't hit extra balls on the course. It is permissible to hit a **provisional ball** if you feel there's a chance that your first ball may not be found. Other than that, however, it is neither appropriate nor allowed to play more than one ball on the course at a time. It is also not fair to other golfers. Get your extra practice on the driving range, not on the course.

If you are slowing the flow on the golf course and there is an open hole in front of you, let the group following play through. If you are playing in a foursome, let a group with two players, for example, play through (unless you aren't delaying them). On extremely busy days, when delays are common, you have no obligation to let groups behind you play through.

Also, when searching for a ball, let other groups play through. If players are waiting and you can't immediately locate your ball, let them play through—don't keep them waiting. In any event, however, do not search for more than two to five minutes for a ball.

Structure your play so the game progresses briskly. Many actions that golfers make add to congestion on the course. If you plan for and play a brisk round of golf, you can cut a lot of time off your game.

Leave the putting green immediately after your group has completed the hole. Record your score on the way to the next hole. If you take time to do it while you're on the green you hold up the group behind you.

Park your cart or leave your bag close to the next tee when on the green. If you have to go back to the front of the green to retrieve your equipment after completing a putt, you hold up the group behind you. Assume you have a short approach shot to the green and are with a partner in a golf cart. You know you will probably need a putter on the next shot, so, to save time, when you get out of the cart take your putter, wedge, and a club you might chip with, while your partner goes on to part the cart near the next tee.

On a par-3 hole, when your group has reached the green, let the next foursome hit from the tee before your group begins to putt. In this way, the trailing party will be walking toward the green while you are putting. That saves time for everyone.

When you begin your game, start at the first hole unless you get permission from the starter to do otherwise. If you start on the 10th hole, you disturb the pattern of flow for players on the first nine holes. This may not be a problem if the course is not busy, but you still must check with the starter.

Help Maintain the Golf Course

Golf is one of the few sports where the player has an important role in maintaining the playing surface. If you ever play on a poorly maintained course with little grass in the teeing area, pitted greens, and fairways full of divot holes, you will readily see the importance of golfer maintenance. Golfers can do a number of things to keep the course from deteriorating.

Don't take more than one practice swing, particularly on the tee. Every time you take a practice swing, you make a small divot, and even if you replace the divot, damage is done. By taking only one practice swing, you reduce such damage.

Replace all divots and repair ball marks. On a well-watered course, a replaced divot will grow into normal grass within a week. An unreplaced divot usually dries out and must be repaired by the grounds crew using sod or soil and seed. Unreplaced divots take many weeks to normalize. If the course is heavily played and many golfers are careless about repairing the damage they do, then the quality of the game decreases for all. On the green, be sure to repair ball marks right away; otherwise they dry out and affect the smoothness of the putting surface.

Rake and smooth out bunkers after using them. A ball that lands in a shoe mark in the bunker must be played as it lies. This makes a difficult shot for the unhappy golfer who hit it there. Give other golfers a break and rake out the trap after you finish using it.

Don't damage the greens. Take care not to damage the greens with improper shoes, by standing on the hole, throwing down the flag, leaning on your putter, or parking a golf cart on it. Greens are very fragile. Damaged greens take a long time to recover.

Don't litter. Wastebaskets are usually located at the tee of each hole. If you can't find one, put your trash in your bag until you do find one. One reason people play golf is to enjoy the outdoors. Littering spoils the view for other golfers.

BASIC RULES OF GOLF

Entire books have been written about the rules of golf. You can get a paperback one from the USGA or any golf shop. It is a good idea to carry a rule book with you as you play. If you don't play by the rules, you aren't playing golf. Playing by the rules gives you a chance to compare your own scores from one round to the next as well as compare yourself with other players—and to do so more accurately.

Try to learn as many rules as possible, turning to the rule book when necessary. However, always keep in mind one guiding principle: Play the ball as it lies and the course as you find it. If you can't do either, do what's fair and reasonable.

Scoring

The two ways to score a golf game are match play and stroke play (sometimes called "medal play"). In **match play,** the score is kept in terms of holes won. The player who wins the most holes wins the match. For example, on the first hole player A scores a 4 and player B scores a 5. Player A wins that hole for getting the lowest score. On the next hole, player B scores a 3 and player A scores a 10. Player B wins this hole and the score is tied, even though player A has many more total strokes than player B. The game continues until one player is more holes ahead than there are holes remaining to be played. Match play is a good way to compete with your friends, particularly if skill levels among you are widely different. A poor score on one hole, such as player A had on the second hole in the example, results in the loss of only that one hole rather than in a gain of seven strokes. If your game is extremely uneven, you may still be involved in the competition during the entire round.

In **stroke play,** you add up the number of strokes for the round and the person with the fewest strokes wins. As discussed in Chapter 2, if people of different ability levels are competing against each other, their handicaps must be subtracted from their scores in order to get a net score.

Rules from the Tee

Players hit their ball from a tee within the teeing ground, a rectangular area two club lengths from front to back bounded on the sides by two tee markers. You are permitted to hit from anywhere within this area, so it's best to select the flattest area with the best footing. You may also stand outside the teeing ground as long as the ball is within it. You may elevate the ball with a tee or by other means. You are not permitted to use a tee outside the teeing ground (that is, on fairways and in bunkers).

A **stroke** has occurred if you move the club forward intending to strike the ball and move it forward. It is not a stroke if the ball falls off the tee and you didn't intend to hit it. However, if you swing at a ball and miss it (whiff), it counts as a stroke.

If you hit a ball and it appears to be out of bounds, to save time you may hit a provisional ball. However, you must first announce that you are playing a provisional ball. If you then find the original ball, you can resume play with it without penalty. If you can't find the original ball, you are assessed a one-stroke penalty for a lost or out-of-bounds ball, in addition to the stroke for the original shot, plus **distance.** Distance means you must rehit from the spot where the ball was first struck. Common penalties in golf are given in Table 6-2.

You are not allowed to take another shot (Mulligans) without penalty just because the first one was unsatisfactory. Taking Mulligans is a bad habit to get into because doing so makes it difficult for you to judge your progress, slows up play—and is against the rules.

TABLE 6-2		
Common Penalties in Golf		
PENALTY	CONSEQUENCE	ACTION
Out of bounds	▪ Two strokes and distance	▪ Hit another ball from where you made original shot.
Lost ball	▪ Two strokes and distance	▪ Hit another ball from where you made original shot.
Playing wrong ball	▪ Two strokes; loss of hole in match play	▪ Return and play correct ball.
Water hazard (WH), horizontal to green (unplayable)	▪ One stroke	▪ Drop behind WH (no limit to how far behind WH ball may be dropped); or play from point of original shot.
WH alongside green (unplayable)	▪ One stroke	▪ Drop two club lengths from point where ball entered hazard or a point on other side of hazard equidistant from the hole.
Unplayable lie (UL)	▪ One stroke	▪ Drop ball two club lengths from UL, no closer to the hole.
Grounding club in hazard	▪ Two strokes; loss of hole in match play	▪ Play ball as it lies.
Striking the flag-stick	▪ Two strokes; loss of hole in match play	▪ Play ball as it lies.
On green, striking other player's ball	▪ Two strokes; no penalty in match play	▪ Player putting plays ball as it lies. Replace hit ball to original position.

Rules from the Fairway

The rules for play on the fairway are complex but need not be intimidating. In general, you must play the ball as it lies. However, there are times when this is not possible—balls can become imbedded in the ground, lost, or hit out of bounds. Beginners should know the basic penalties and exceptions to this rule of play the ball as it lies and the course as you find it (see Tables 6-2 and 6-3).

The exceptions to playing the ball as it lies are very specific. When one of these situations arises, you are allowed **relief**—that is, allowed to drop the ball without penalty—but you must follow a certain procedure. In general, you must drop the ball as near as possible to the place where it lay (for example, an unplayable lie). Face the green, with your arm extended shoulder high to the side or in front, and drop the ball—but not closer to the hole (see Figure 6-2). Drop the ball again if it rolls closer to the fairway, hits you as it drops, goes out of bounds or into a hazard, or if it falls more than two club lengths from the original spot.

TABLE 6-3	
Exceptions to Playing the Ball as It Lies and the Course as You Find It	
CONDITION	ACTION
Local variations of rules ("winter rules"). Examples: obstructions, ground under repair, temporary conditions, roads and paths, etc.	Local option. Usually, drop ball two club lengths from condition.
Casual water, ground under repair, hole made by burrowing animal	Drop at nearest point not affected by condition (within one club length) and no closer to the hole.
Casual water in your line while on the putting green	Move to nearest ground that provides relief that is the same distance from the hole.
Movable obstruction (artificial, not considered natural part of the course)	Any movable obstruction (objects affecting stance or swing, or those in line of play) may be removed.
Immovable obstruction (artificial)	Player is entitled to relief only if object interferes with stance or swing. No relief if object is in line of play.
Cleaning or marking ball that is on the green	Mark ball, clean, and replace without penalty.
Removal of loose impediments on putting green	Players may move loose dirt, sand, twigs, and other loose impediments from green (only with hand or club).
Repair of ball marks on green	Players may repair ball marks on green. Players may not repair spike marks or push down raised clumps of grass until hole is completed.

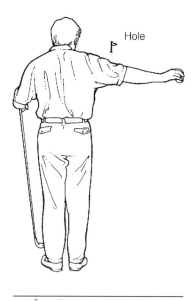

Hole

Figure 6-2
How to drop a ball on the course.
Stand, facing the hole with your
arm extended straight to the side,
and drop the ball.

You are entitled to relief if a ball is imbedded in its own pitch mark. You are allowed to lift the ball from the fairway or rough and drop it, without penalty, as near as possible to the place where it was imbedded (but, as noted, not closer to the hole). You may not move your ball if it lands in a divot or is imbedded in the rough.

You may not manipulate any part of the course that is considered natural to improve your lie or line of play. This means that you can't break branches, remove dirt or sand, cut down grass, or smooth out depressions in the ground. Play the course as you find it!

There are many exceptions to this rule. Most courses have local variations that allow you relief for shots that land in ground under repair, on roads, or in piles of leaves. These exceptions are clearly specified and should not be used as an excuse to improve your lie whenever it suits you. Don't be one of those players who uses "winter rules" (local variations) all year long. The United States Golf Association discourages using winter rules* for several reasons:

1. Winter rules violate the basic principle of playing the ball where it lies.

2. Rather than protecting the course, the rules encourage golfers to hit from the best turf.

3. Winter rules improve scores and lower handicaps, which penalizes players when they play against golfers who established their handicaps under the USGA Rules of Golf.

4. Regular use of winter rules places you at a disadvantage when you play a match that requires you to play the ball as it lies.

You are allowed relief for **casual water, ground under repair,** and for holes made by burrowing animals. Casual water is water, ice, or snow that is not part of a water hazard. Frost and dew are not casual water. As a general rule, the water must rise above the soles of your shoes when you stand in it for it to be classified as casual water. Soft ground and mud are not necessarily classified as casual water. You are allowed to drop the ball at one club length from the original lie (but not nearer the hole) in a spot that avoids interference with the condition (that is, the casual water) and is

*USGA Rules of Golf, 1992, p. 104.

not in a hazard or on a putting green. You are allowed to clean the ball when taking relief.

You may move any movable obstruction. An **obstruction** is anything artificial that is not considered an integral part of the course. Movable obstructions may include benches, hoses, and rakes. You are allowed relief from an immovable obstruction only if it disturbs your stance or swing. You are not entitled to relief if it is in the line of play. An out-of-bounds fence, for example, is not considered an obstruction. If your ball is resting on the fence, you must either play it or declare it unplayable.

You are not allowed to play a ball that landed on the wrong green. Although local rules may differ slightly, in general, place the ball one club length from the nearest point off the green, no closer to the hole. There is no penalty. Practice putting greens also fall under this provision of the rules.

You are responsible for playing the right ball. Playing a wrong ball is a two-stroke penalty. If the ball belongs to one of your current competitors, its owner must replace the ball, hitting it from the place where it was improperly hit. A good practice is to mark your ball with a felt-tip pen so you can positively identify it.

You may lift a ball from the fairway for identification, provided you announce your intention to your competitors. You are allowed to clean the ball only when necessary for identification. There is a one-stroke penalty for cleaning a ball more than necessary for identification, unless the ball was recovered from an imbedded lie, standing water, or an unplayable lie. You are allowed to clean a ball that is on the putting green. You are not allowed to pick up or clean a ball in a hazard. If a ball is covered with sand, you are allowed to brush enough sand off of it so it can be seen.

On the green you are allowed more leeway with the ball and playing surface than on the fairway. You may mark and clean your ball, but the ball must be replaced in the exact spot when the time is appropriate. You may repair ball marks and remove loose impediments (sand, twigs, cigarette butts, etc.) in the path of your ball. You may not smooth out contour irregularities caused by clumps of grass or spike marks. You are allowed to concede a putt to your opponent in match play but not in stroke play. Disqualification is the penalty for failure to "hole out" in stroke play.

Common Penalties

Many penalties in golf are difficult to understand, even for experienced golfers. There are penalties for using too many clubs, seeking advice from other players, and having another player or caddie stand in the line of play when you're playing. There is even a penalty for agreeing to violate the rules. In stroke play, if you concede a putt to an opponent, you are technically in violation of the rules.

Out of Bounds (OB)   You are prohibited from playing on ground designated as out of bounds. **Out of bounds** is outside the golf course. It may be someone's front lawn or a farmer's pasture, and you may be trespassing if you attempt it. Out of bounds is marked by white stakes or a fence. The penalty for hitting a ball out of bounds is strokes and distance: one stroke for the ball you hit, a penalty stroke, and hitting the ball from your original location. You are not permitted to drop the ball near where it went out of bounds. As discussed, if you are not sure the ball is out of bounds, then you can hit a provisional ball to save time.

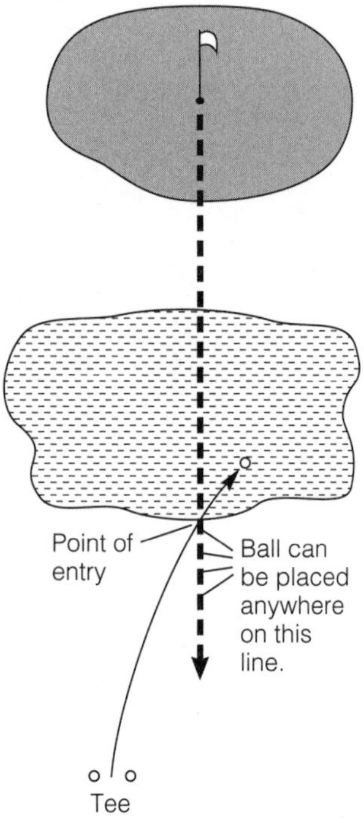

Lost Ball   A **lost ball** is treated like a ball hit out of bounds. You are not allowed to hit the ball from a place you approximate the ball was lost. You must shoot from the original place you shot when you lost the ball (distance penalty). If you hit the ball deep into a clump of trees and have little hope of finding it, hit a provisional ball. When you confirm that you lost the ball, count all strokes taken, add a penalty stroke, and continue playing with the provisional ball.

Water Hazard   If your ball lands in a water hazard and you think it unplayable, you are assessed one penalty stroke. If the hazard lies horizontally across the fairway between you and the green, you drop the ball behind the hazard (that is, on the side away from the green) anywhere along a line that runs directly from the point of entry to the hole (Figure 6-3). If you hit a ball into a hazard that lies alongside (lateral to) the green and the fairway, drop the ball two club lengths from the point where the ball entered the hazard or at a point on the other side of the hazard that is either in line with the point of entry or is equidistant to the hole (Figure 6-4). You may play a ball out of a water hazard but you may not ground the club (water or sand) in doing so. Grounding the club will cost you two strokes in stroke play and loss of the hole in match play.

Unplayable Lie   The golfer determines if a ball rests in an unplayable lie (except when the ball is in a water hazard). If it is, take a one-stroke penalty. Then play the ball as close as possible to the site of the unplayable lie (no closer to the hole), dropping it within two club lengths of the unplayable lie (no closer to the

Figure 6-3
Procedure for placing the ball on the fairway when you hit into a water hazard that lies horizontally across the fairway between you and the green. You may place the ball anywhere on the line behind the point of entry.

hole), or behind the point of the unplayable lie (there is no limit as to how far behind). In all options, you must keep the point at which the ball is unplayable between you and the hole. You are allowed to clean the ball when moving it from an unplayable lie.

Playing the Wrong Ball   The penalty for playing the wrong ball is two strokes. Also, you must return to the location of the correct ball and play out the hole. As part of this rule, you are prohibited from switching balls in the middle of a hole. Many golfers use older balls for playing on the fairway and new balls for putting. This is against the rules.

Putting Green Penalties   On the putting green, there are two penalties of which you should be particularly aware. If you take a shot from the green and it strikes the flagstick, you are assessed a penalty of two strokes in stroke play and loss of the hole in a match play. There is no penalty for hitting the flagstick if your shot was from off the green. In stroke play, when putting from the green, if you hit someone else's ball, the penalty is two strokes. The ball you hit is returned to its original place on the green and you must play your ball where it lies.

REFERENCES

United States Golf Association. *The Rules of Golf.* Far Hills, NJ: The United States Golf Association and The Royal and Ancient Golf Club of St. Andrews, Scotland, 1992.

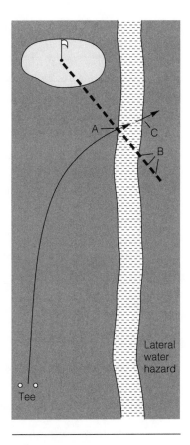

Figure 6-4
Procedure for placing the ball on the fairway when you hit into a water hazard that lies alongside the fairway and the green. You may play the ball at the point of entry (A), play the ball on the other side of the water hazard in line with the point of entry (B), or play the ball on the other side of the water hazard at an equal distance from the hole (C) as the point of entry.

Worksheet

1. Golf etiquette includes three basic principles: _____
   _____
   _____

2. Shout _____ if a player on the course is in danger of being hit by your ball.

3. _____ is the privilege of playing first from the teeing ground.

4. If you are slowing the flow on the golf course what should you do? _____
   _____

5. How can you help maintain the golf course? _____
   _____
   _____
   _____

6. The two ways to score a golf game are _____ and _____.

7. If you hit a ball and it appears that it might be out of bounds, to save time you may hit a
   _____ ball.

8. What is the penalty for hitting the ball out of bounds? _____
   _____

9. A(n) _____ is anything artificial that is not considered an integral part of the course.

10. What is the penalty for hitting the wrong ball? _____

11. What is the penalty for hitting the flagstick from the green? _____

CHAPTER 7

Golf and Your Body

Why is a chapter on conditioning and athletic injuries included in a golf book? First, golfers—like everyone else—need exercise to stay healthy. Golf can contribute to your physical fitness—if you walk the course rather than ride a cart and don't become hampered by injuries. Integrate golf into a total fitness and nutrition program that stresses endurance, strength, and flexibility exercises and a well-balanced, low-fat diet. If you ride a cart when you play, eat junk food and drink alcoholic beverages while at the course, and become injured because you are unfit, then golf may have a negative effect on your health.

Second, this chapter is included because golfers suffer from a surprising number of sometimes incapacitating injuries. A recent study of amateur golfers showed that 62 percent had sustained an injury while playing or practicing for the sport. The most common sites of injury were the back, wrist, elbow, shoulder, and knee (Figure 7-1). Most experts agree that an underlying reason for most of these injuries is lack of conditioning and poor mechanics during the golf swing.

This chapter discusses the contributions of golf to fitness and the physical requirements of the sport, as well as common golf injuries and how to prevent them.

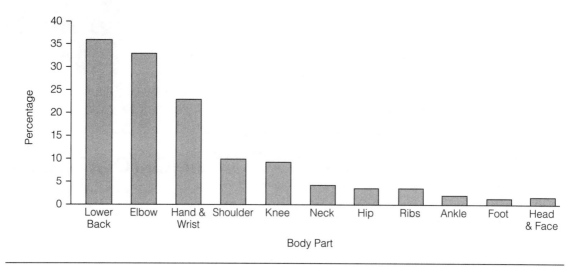

Figure 7-1
Common injuries in golf. Adapted from: J. R. McCarroll, A. C. Rettig, and K. D. Shelbourne, "Injuries in the amateur golfer," *Physician Sportsmed.* 18 (1990): 122-126.

HOW MUCH EXERCISE DO YOU NEED?

Over 50 percent of all deaths in Western countries is due to heart disease. Physical fitness reduces the risk of heart disease. The American College of Sports Medicine and the American Heart Association make the following recommendations:

- *Do endurance exercises that work major muscle groups, continuously, for a long period.* The best exercises for the cardiovascular system are walking, running, cycling, swimming, and cross-country skiing. Other good exercises for cardiovascular fitness include tennis, basketball, and racquetball. However, to benefit from these "start-and-stop sports," you must be skilled and play for at least 30–60 minutes. Golf meets this requirement if you walk the course and carry your bag.

- *Exercise above 50 percent of maximum capacity.* Golf is not an ideal aerobic exercise because it is not strenuous enough. However, you can increase the intensity of exercise during a golf game by walking briskly on the fairways. (As an added bonus, you do a service to other golfers by speeding up play.)

- *Exercise for 15–60 minutes a session.* Golf can satisfy this training requirement. It usually takes at least three hours to play 18 holes of golf. Although you are not exercising continuously during a round of golf, you do a lot of walking.

- *Exercise three to six days a week.* Many people don't have time to play golf three to six times a week, so other kinds of exercise must be included in the fitness program to get enough exercise. A variety of fitness activities adds interest and will ultimately improve your golf game. For example, you will tire less easily when you play, which will give you a more consistent swing. Also, because your overall fitness is better, you will be less susceptible to injury.

Will golf satisfy your exercise requirements? Because most golfers don't walk very fast, golf should not be the only kind of aerobic exercise you do. However, if you walk briskly, the game can contribute to good health: You get some aerobic benefits, and you profit from the relaxation golf provides.

Golf and Heart Disease

Few studies have examined the effects of golf on health. However, indirect evidence shows that golf is good for you. Walking, even walking slowly, reduces the risk of heart disease (see the references at the end of the chapter). Walking decreases anxiety and tension, improves aerobic capacity, reduces cholesterol, increases a substance in the blood that scavenges cholesterol (HDL2), increases muscle mass, decreases body fat, and increases bone mineral content in post-menopausal women.

In walking studies, subjects typically exercise continuously for at least 30 minutes during each workout. Because, during a round of golf, you don't walk continuously, you lose some of the benefits of walking as an exercise. You make up for this, however, by carrying your bag and clubs while walking the course.

The amount of physical activity you do each week is as important as the intensity of the activity. Merely doing something active three to five days a week provides almost the same protection against heart disease as more intense regular training.

If you walk 18 holes, you will walk more than 3 miles—particularly if you don't hit the ball straight every time. If the course is also hilly, the energy expended during the round can be considerable. Again, from the standpoint of prevention of heart disease, playing golf (walking and carrying your clubs) contributes to your health. More important, you reduce stress as well as get the enjoyment and camaraderie that comes with playing golf.

Are golfers fit? Studies of professional golfers show that, unfortunately, they are not very fit. They are about as fit as the typical sedentary person of their age. However, better golfers usually have better aerobic capacity and muscle strength than less skilled golfers.

Golf and Injuries

There is good evidence that being in shape prevents injuries and allows you to play golf better. Fit golfers have better stamina, strength, and flexibility than unfit players. You can practice more when you are fit. Motor learning scientists (people who study how we learn physical skills) have shown that you can learn movement skills, such as the golf swing, much better when you are fresh than when you are fatigued. Tired, out-of-shape golfers practice faulty movement patterns that can become bad habits, replacing the good habits of correct golfing techniques.

Injuries rather than old age often end the playing careers of athletes. After an injury, the body heals itself by laying down scar tissue, which is tough and not very elastic. Healthy tissue around a scar is subject to unusual stress and is itself more subject to injury in the future. As you sustain a series of small injuries over a lifetime, you gradually lose capacity in the injured areas.

You can combat this process by preventing injuries in the first place. Rehabilitate injuries—that is, stretch and strengthen injured tissues—as much as possible so you don't get hurt in the same place again. For the golfer, this means improving fitness in parts of the body that are often injured in golf. Do abdominal and back exercises to protect the back. Do upper body exercises to strengthen the rotator cuff muscles of the shoulders and muscles of the upper and lower arms. Run, walk, cycle, and train with weights to develop strong legs to prevent injuries to the knees and ankles.

Whether you are concerned about your health or just want to play better golf, it makes good sense to improve your fitness. When you are in shape, your game becomes more consistent, you suffer fewer injuries, and, in general, you are a healthier person.

Other Hazards in Golf

Natural hazards, including lightning, sun, and insects, cause a surprisingly high number of problems for golfers. The severity of these problems ranges from minor to life threatening.

Lightning   When people want to describe a freak, chance occurrence, they say, "It's like being struck by lightning." Lee

Trevino, the great professional golfer, has been struck by lightning twice in his career. If you play golf where there is a lot of thunderstorm activity, you increase your risk of being struck. A golf club acts as a lightning rod and will attract lightning to you.

Lightning is an electrical current that tries to cross the gap between a cloud and the ground. It follows the line of least resistance and will travel through a conductor instead of air in its attempt to reach ground. For this reason, the tallest object on the golf course is at greatest risk of being struck by lightning. A golfer holding a metal club (an excellent conductor of electricity) is often the highest object. Following are a few guidelines for avoiding lightning strikes on the golf course:

- Get off the course if lightning occurs.
- Stay away from trees. Trees are poor conductors of electricity. If lightning strikes a tree, current may flash from its sides and strike you.
- Go to a low point on the course, such as a ditch.
- Get into a steel structure or automobile. These are well insulated and provide a good path for electricity to go to ground.
- Don't tempt lightning—move to safety immediately!

Golf and Flexibility

Flexibility is the ability to move the joints through their capability range. The capability range is a joint's maximum range of motion. People with good flexibility can twist their trunks and extend their shoulders more than those who are less flexible. Golf requires extreme movements. During the takeaway part of the swing, the trunk twists almost to its fullest extent. As the swing progresses, the trunk twists completely in the opposite direction. The flexibility ranges of shoulders, hips, knees, and ankles are also pushed close to the limit during the golf swing. You can injure inflexible muscles during the quick and powerful movements of the golf swing.

You often tax the limits of flexibility during a golf game. By working the joints through a large range of motion, you either maintain or develop flexibility. Good flexibility is beneficial to golfers. Flexible golfers can perform a smooth, relaxed swing, with one part of the action moving easily into the next. Smooth, coordinated movements lead to consistency in your swing—and consistency is one of the keys to getting good scores and dropping strokes.

Include stretching exercises as a regular part of your day. You don't need to become a stretching fanatic. Even a few minutes of stretching exercises a day can help you maintain or improve flexibility and prevent common golf injuries. Follow these guidelines to get the most benefit from stretching exercises:

- Perform stretching exercises statically—that is stretch and hold the position for 10 to 30 seconds.
- Stretch until you feel a minor tug rather than pain. Relax when you do stretching exercises.
- Avoid positions that increase the risk of low-back injury. For example, when performing straight leg, toe-touching exercises, bend your knees slightly as you return to a standing position.
- As with other forms of physical conditioning, develop flexibility gradually over time.
- There are big differences among individuals in joint flexibility. Do not compete with other people during stretching workouts.
- Practice flexibility exercises as least five days a week. Set aside a special time to work on them.
- Stretch before you play golf. Although pregolf stretching will usually not be as thorough as a stretching workout, you should at least stretch the major muscles and joints used during the golf swing.

PREVENTING GOLF INJURIES

Prevent golf injuries by being physically fit, by properly warming up before practicing or playing a round of golf, and by developing a smooth, mechanically correct swing. Fitness prevents stress to the back, arms, shoulders, and knees. If you are in good shape, you get less tired during a round of golf and so can maintain good technique while you play; you are also less likely to get injured. Warm-up exercises contribute to injury prevention by lubricating joints, increasing the pliability of joints, and directing blood to exercising muscles. Good technique means a smooth transition between different parts of the golf swing; poor technique leads to jerky movements that can damage muscles and joints.

Exercising to develop fitness and prevent injuries should include endurance exercises for stamina, strength exercises to develop muscles critical to power, and flexibility exercises to expand the range of motion in muscles and joints during the swing. As noted earlier, endurance is best developed through activities other than golf. Practice regularly activities such as running, walking (continuous walking at a fast pace), swimming, and cycling. Do strength exercises that develop the muscles of the shoulders, arms, back, abdomen, and legs. Do flexibility exercises that emphasize the spine, shoulders, hips, and knees.

Warm-Up

A warm-up session is very important for golfers, but it is often ignored. A warm-up session offers the following benefits:

- *Increased muscle temperature.* Muscles work better when their temperature is slightly higher than when at rest. Doing a few range-of-motion exercises or even going for a short run before you play will increase muscle temperature and make your muscles work more efficiently.

- *Increased joint lubrication.* Joints are lubricated with a substance called synovial fluid. This fluid is important because it supplies oxygen and fuels to the cartilage cells that line the joint's surface. Movement disburses the fluid throughout the joint, thus reducing the risk of joint injury.

- *Increased circulation to exercising muscles.* Adequate blood flow is important for preventing injury. When you are at rest, a relatively small portion of the body's blood supply resides in the muscles. During exercise, most of the body's blood is found there. Warming up helps speed the redistribution of blood to the muscles, which may help prevent injury. However, warm-up exercises must be more than 50 percent of maximum (your maximum exercise intensity) to have much of an effect on muscle circulation.

- *Opportunity to practice.* Hitting a bucket of balls before playing golf not only provides specific warm-up for your golf muscles, it allows additional practice that helps you focus on good technique. Good technique, characterized by a smooth transition from one part of the golf swing to the next, is critical to injury prevention. Be sure to do stretching and general joint warm-up exercises before hitting balls.

- When hitting practice balls, warm up with your short irons first (wedge, 8, and 9) before progressing to the longer irons and woods. Warm up intelligently: Pick a target and try to get as close to it as possible. Emphasize good technique on every shot. Relax and try to move smoothly between the different parts of the swing. Don't try to intimidate your partners by hitting the ball as far as possible. Golf is a game of accuracy. Save displays of power for the baseball field or weight room.

Warm-Up Exercises for Golf

The three basic types of warm-up exercises for golf are stretching, general joint mobility exercises, and practice shots on the driving range. Each type of exercise provides some of the same benefits as the others—but each provides distinct advantages as well. Arrive at the course early enough to do your warm-up exercises. It is difficult to hit a bucket of balls if your foursome is next up on the tee. Give yourself enough warm-up time so your body is ready for the round and your mind is focused on the game.

Don't be self-conscious about warming up at the driving range. If people look at you strangely, remember that they will be the ones who get injured and not you.

Stretching   Golfers should do stretching exercises for the hamstrings (muscles on the back of the legs), quadriceps (muscles on the front of the legs), Achilles tendon (cord between calf and heel), trunk, shoulders, and forearms. These exercises take only about two to three minutes to do and will loosen you up before you play. Good stretching exercises are shown in Figure 7-2.

General Joint Mobility   Warm-up exercises for general joint mobility are important for joint lubrication, increasing blood flow to muscles and the heart, and increasing muscle temperature (which will make you more powerful). One-arm swings are especially good for warming up muscle groups important in golf (Figure 7-3).

Practice Shots on the Driving Range and Practice Swings on the Tee   Pregame practice is important for getting physically and mentally prepared for the round. Before a match, professional golfers usually take about 50 shots with irons and drivers and 30–50 putts. Preround practice gets your mind on the game and helps you iron out last-minute glitches in your swing. If the course you are going to play has a practice range, use it. If not, find one nearby and use that before showing up for your round. The time is well spent.

Start your warm-up with shorter irons (the 7–9 irons), then progress to the longer irons and woods. Take easy swings and

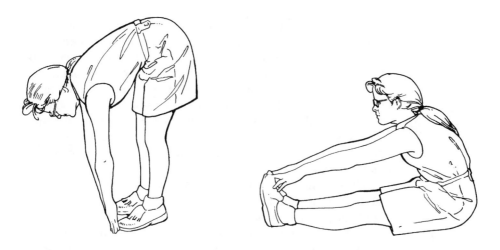

Figure 7-2
Hamstring exercises.

Figure 7-3
One-arm golf swings are an excellent way to warm up muscles
you will use when playing golf.

work for consistency. Concentrate on each stroke. Before you swing, picture a successful and fluid swing in your mind. Try to relax. The warm-up period can be very helpful in getting you from the stresses of daily life to concentration on your golf game.

Take a few chips at the green before putting. When taking practice putts, start with basic "bread-and-butter" 3–6 foot shots and then gradually increase the distance. Take some putts on irregular surfaces to get a feel for green speed. The condition of the practice green can often tell you something about the green speed on the course.

Taking practice swings at the tee is also an effective way to warm up (although not as effective as taking shots at the range). Do your practice swings off the tee itself, however—making divots on the tee contributes to excessive course wear. Take your practice swings away from other people. You can easily hit someone with your club or, if people are in the line of fire, with a divot, twig, or other object—even a clubhead that happens to come loose from the shaft.

DEVELOPING STRENGTH FOR GOLF

Weight training is extremely effective for golf. Weight training can help you hit the ball harder and with more authority—but not overhit it when you have a long shot. Knowing you have plenty of power to hit the ball allows you to take a relaxed swing.

Golf requires lower body explosiveness, powerful abdominal muscles and back muscles, and strong arms and shoulders. Because injuries to the back are common among golfers, all golfers should do exercises to help prevent them.

A detailed discussion of weight training is beyond the scope of this book. However, a basic weight training program appropriate for golfers is given in Table 7-1. Two basic terms used in the table are *repetitions,* the number of times an exercise is done during a set, and *sets,* a group of repetitions followed by rest. The best strength building program develops all of the body's major muscle groups but emphasizes critical areas such as the trunk and forearms. Golfers interested in weight training to improve their game and personal fitness should do the exercises in the program two to three days a week. Get advice from an exercise leader or coach before beginning a weight training program. If you are unsure if weight training is medically appropriate for you, see your physician.

TABLE 7-1		
A Basic Weight Training Program for Golf		
EXERCISE	SETS	REPETITIONS
Bench press	3	10
Lat pulls	3	10
Biceps curls	3	10
Triceps extensions	3	10
Abdominal curls	3	10
Twists	3	10
Squats	3	10
Knee extensions	3	10
Leg curls	3	10
Wrist extensions/flexions	3	10
Back extensions	3	10
Isometric back exercise	3	10

Weight training books, such as *Basic Weight Training* and *Basic Weight Training for Women* (Mayfield Publishing) give detailed discussions of weight training methods.

Golf is an excellent game that can contribute to your health, fitness, and well-being. You will enjoy the game more and prevent injuries if you stay in good shape by regularly doing endurance, strength, and flexibility exercises.

REFERENCES

American College of Sports Medicine. *Guidelines for Exercise Testing and Prescription*. Philadelphia: Lea & Febiger, 1991.

Blair, S. N., and H. W. Kohl. "Physical activity or physical fitness: Which is more important for health?" *Med. Sci. Sports Exerc.* 20 (1988): S8.

Crews, D. "A physiological profile of ladies professional golf association tour players." *Physician Sportsmed.* 12 (1984): 69–74.

Duda, M. "Golfers use exercise to get back in the swing." *Physician Sportsmed.* 17 (1989): 109–113.

Jobe, F. W., and D. R. Moynes. *30 Exercises for Better Golf*. Inglewood, CA: Champion Press, 1986.

Jobe, F. W., D. R. Moynes, and D. J. Antonelli. "Rotator cuff function during a golf swing." *Am. J. Sports Med.* 14 (1986): 388–392.

Lauria, M. H., and K. R. Koepke. "The physical conditioning effects of walking." *J. Sports Medicine* 15 (1975): 272–274.

McCarroll, J. R., and T. J. Gioe. "Professional golfers and the price they pay." *Physician Sportsmed.* 10 (1982): 64–70.

McCarroll, J. R., A. C. Rettig, and K. D. Shelbourne. "Injuries in the amateur golfer." *Physician Sportsmed.* 18 (1990): 122–126.

O'Grady, R., and D. Shoch. "Golf-ball granuloma of the eyelids and conjuctiva." *Am. J. Ophthalmol.* 76 (1973): 148–151.

Porcari, J. P., C. B. Ebbeling, A. Ward, P. S. Freedson, and J. M. Rippe. "Walking for exercise testing and training." *Sports Medicine* 8 (1989): 189–200.

Rippe, J. M., A. Ward, and P. S. Freedson. "Walking: Nothing pedestrian about it." In *1988 Medical Health Annual.* Chicago: Encyclopaedia Britannica, 1987.

Safran, M. R., A. V. Seaber, and W. E. Garrett. "Warm-up and muscular injury prevention." *Sports Medicine* 8 (1989): 239–249.

Schulenburg, C. A. "Medical aspects and curiosities of golfing." *Practitioner* 217 (1976): 625–628.

Stover, C. N., G. Wiren, and S. R. Topaz. "The modern golf swing and stress syndromes." *Physician Sportsmed.* 4 (1976): 42–47.

Vallotton, W. W. "The ocular aspects of golf." *South Med. J.* 58 (1965): 44–47.

Voss, M. W. "A medical support system for a professional golf tournament." *Physician Sportsmed.* 10 (1982): 63–70.

Weston, P. A. "Injury from disrupted golf ball." *Lancet* 1, no. 8007 (1977): 375.

Williams, K. R., and P. R. Cavanagh. "Mechanics of foot action during the golf swing and implications for shoe design." *Med. Sci. Sports Exerc.* 15 (1983): 247–255.

Worksheet

1. What's a good endurance exercise prescription for the average person? _____

    _____

    _____

    _____

    _____

2. What types of fitness are important for golfers? _____

    _____

3. What are some benefits of warming up? _____

    _____

    _____

    _____

Conditioning the Mind for Golf

The mental aspects of golf have been the target of comedians and cartoonists for years. Typical cartoons show a distraught golfer who made a bad shot in a state of rage, wrapping his club around a tree or breaking it over his knee. The mental frustrations of golf led Oscar Wilde, the famous English playwright, to define golf as a walk in the country, spoiled.

The frustrations of the game are based on its structure: Every time you make a mistake, it becomes more difficult to get a good score. In golf, every poor shot adds to your score and stays with you for the entire game. In games such as tennis or volleyball, you can make mistakes but recover if you play reasonably well for the remainder of the game. In golf, however, every added stroke diminishes the quality of your game.

An important part of golf's mental aspect is not to let bad shots disturb you. If you do, one bad shot will lead to other bad shots. Many golfers get so upset when they make bad shots that they lose concentration and dwell on previous errors, thus ruining the rest of their game.

Although you need exacting physical skills to get a good score, golf is largely a mental game. To be successful, you must continually study the course, concentrate on technique, and avoid distractions. Mastering the mental aspects of the game is as important as becoming proficient in the physical skills. This chapter summarizes some important mental strategies that will make you a better golfer.

SUCCESS IN GOLF DEMANDS DISCIPLINE AND EMOTIONAL TOUGHNESS

Psychological studies of successful golfers have found that, with few exceptions, they are extremely stable emotionally. Successful golfers are achievement-oriented people who derive personal satisfaction from striving. High achievement needs are based on personal attitudes about the probability of success or failure of each investment of self or ego. All things considered, outstanding golfers are at their best when the odds are slightly against them. Ambitious people are happiest when their abilities are challenged. Great golfers do not dwell on losses but concentrate on that part of their performance that limits their excellence. The nature of golf demands that the good player, whether amateur or professional, be extremely calm under pressure and unaffected by distractions.

Bruce Ogilvie, perhaps the best known sports psychologist in the world, identified differences in character between successful and unsuccessful athletes in a variety of sports, including golf. He noted that successful athletes are almost completely free of physical fear. In golf, this means not being afraid to fail. For example, a mentally tough golfer will sink most 3–6 foot putts without thinking about it. Golfers who have not mastered the mental part of the game will have doubts. They will think, "What if I miss this putt? If I miss this putt, I will embarrass myself in front of my friends!" In this state of mind, fears often become self-fulfilling prophecies and you miss the putt. As they say on the sports shoe commercials, "Just do it!"

A mentally tough golfer can make a bad shot, forget about it, and do well on the next shot. Good golfers must concentrate and reduce distractions, as well as look for opportunities during the game to improve the score. An old saying in golf is that given equality of strength and skill, victory in golf will go to the person who is captain of his soul.

THE THREE MENTAL ELEMENTS OF SUCCESS IN GOLF: BELIEF, VISION, AND METHOD

The psychological tenacity necessary for success in golf includes three simple elements: belief, vision, and method. Belief is self-confidence—knowing your worth as a golfer and believing you can do well. Vision is your goal—you have to know what you want to get. Method is the process you use to fulfill your vision—how you practice and how you handle yourself in the pressure and excitement of a golf game.

Developing Belief in Your Abilities as a Golfer

Belief means having confidence in your abilities and in your capacity to learn to play golf. Self-confidence is perhaps the most important mental attribute a golfer can have. If you don't have it, becoming a good golfer will be difficult. You must take the attitude that if you consistently make the same mistake on the course, you have not learned certain important skills. It's not that you can't learn the skill or you are innately uncoordinated. Rather, there are simply a few skills you haven't yet learned. You must say to yourself, I haven't learned these skills yet, but I will.

Self-confidence takes a long time to develop; it's something you have to learn. Self-confidence is based on accomplishment, and you develop it by succeeding in a series of short-term goals. As you experience several small victories, you begin to realize that nothing is impossible. Then, the only thing stopping you from getting what you want is yourself. If you don't believe you can do something, there's no way you will do it. Confidence, or belief, is the cornerstone of athletic success—or success in anything.

A look at some of the heroes of history shows the power of belief. People such as Christopher Columbus, George Washington, and Abraham Lincoln succeeded because of an unswerving belief that they were on the right track. Likewise, great golfers, such as Babe Didrikson-Zaharias, Arnold Palmer, Jack Nicklaus, Tom Watson, Nancy Lopez, and Patty Berg, are characterized by their self-confidence. You need to have a strong belief in your abilities. Let nothing get in your way. Believe in yourself. If you keep hammering away at your goal, you will succeed!

On the golf course, be self-confident, even if you are a beginner and have no reason to be. Confidence makes your movement patterns smoother and less jerky. If you are trying to sink a 5-foot putt, do it with confidence, even if your skills are minimal. Off the tee, think briefly about your drive, then move to the tee, address the ball, and hit it. Don't let negative thoughts enter your mind. A positive mental attitude will save you strokes regardless of your skill level.

Developing Vision

Although you may not have the time, talent, or inclination to become a great golfer, you can probably become competent at the game if you put out a little effort. If you are systematic and use your practice and time on the golf course effectively, you can become a good golfer without spending all your time working on the game. If you are going to put in eight hours every couple of weeks playing golf, why not achieve some success at it? With a little structure you can turn that time into something that improves your game and makes it more enjoyable.

Set small goals that you can achieve. Gradually, these small achievements will become major accomplishments. Achieving a series of small successes is the secret to success of all athletes involved in individual sports. They develop their skills gradually over a long time. You can do the same by taking it one small step at a time.

Let a good and caring instructor help you with the basics: developing a good grip, balanced body position, proper turn, natural weight shift, smooth swing, and complete follow-through. Learn the basics of proper course management: which clubs to play in given situations, where to hit the ball to avoid trouble, how to read greens, and how to assess the effects of wind. Once you have established a good foundation, you will find that improving your game is not difficult. You can also more clearly determine your goals for the future.

Assess your goals and desires realistically. If you don't want to be a professional golfer, be happy with whatever accomplishments you make. Don't downgrade them. Assess your weaknesses and work to improve them. Don't limit yourself. At first, it may seem that breaking 110 is impossible. However, after you develop some basic techniques and play more consistently, you may quickly move to the 90s, 80s, or even the 70s. Golf is not difficult once you get the hang of it.

Method: The Key To Becoming a Good Golfer

Method is the process by which you achieve your goals. Most golfers are familiar with the physical methods of the game. Obviously, a lot of hard work is necessary to achieve top-level success. However, mental agility is also necessary for that kind of achievement. Efficient practice sessions, good golf course management (strategy you use during a game), coachability, and a good psychological approach to the game are critical to becoming a good golfer.

PSYCHOLOGICAL PRINCIPLES IMPORTANT FOR SUCCESS IN GOLF

Probably the most important psychological principle for success in golf is to become more systematic. Golf is a game of consistency. Although conditions vary slightly from shot to shot, the golf swing is almost always the same with every club (except the putter, of course). Consider your body to be like a lump of clay that you are going to mold into championship form. If you are systematic, you will eventually be successful. A number of mental principles will help you become a better golfer (Table 8-1).

Find a Good Coach or Golf Instructor   This principle was first discussed in Chapter 2. It is critical to becoming a good golfer and enjoying the game to the fullest. Getting a good coach should be the first thing you do, even before buying equipment, hitting a bucket of balls, or playing a round of golf. It is very easy to develop bad habits in golf. Too many people buy a cheap set of clubs at the local sports discount store and then start playing. The clubs are seldom adequate for your body build or swing and you have a handicap before you begin. Inevitably, you develop bad habits that are extremely difficult to break, even when you do seek good coaching. A good coach will teach you the fundamentals of the sport, support you emotionally, and help you direct your progression in learning to play golf.

Your skill level determines the expertise of the coach you need. If you are new to the game, it is not important to have an instructor who usually works with pros. All you need is someone who knows the fundamentals of golf and can help you with your program and your progress. That's not to say you should enlist the help of your next door neighbor who once broke 100. Get an experienced, knowledgeable instructor.

As noted earlier, you can get coaching by taking a golf class in college or taking lessons from the pro at the local golf course or driving range. The coach will help you develop good techniques and can make suggestions on the best equipment for your body type and golf swing. The coach will also help you outline a step-by-step procedure for taking you from where you are now to where you want to go.

TABLE 8-1

Important Mental Principles of Golf

- Find a good coach or instructor.
- Find people to play golf with.
- Keep calm.
- Be optimistic.
- Be confident.
- Concentrate!
- Don't let bad shots or bad breaks get you down.
- Don't try to overcompensate for a bad shot.
- Don't try to change your swing in the middle of a round.
- Play every shot to the best of your ability.
- Always look for opportunities to save strokes.
- Picture successful shots.
- Don't overanalyze your game.
- Never give up.
- Play the percentages.
- Develop a routine.
- Stress quality when you practice.
- Play by the rules.
- Keep up on the latest techniques.
- Have fun!

Find People to Play Golf With   Although golf is an individual sport, it is much more fun to play it with a group of friends. Developing golfing relationships will encourage you to go to the course or practice range more often. Also, golfing friends provide the competitive atmosphere necessary to improving your game.

Find people who play at or slightly above your skill level. Your partners should complement your personality and help you compensate for your psychological shortcomings in learning to play the game. If you need to be pushed, find people who are enthusiastic and will push you to new limits. If you are anxious and overbearing in your approach to golf, find people who will calm you down.

Keep Calm   Emotionally, golf is like a roller coaster. You spend most of the time walking or riding on the course, lining up your shots, and anticipating your next move. The stress is similar to that experienced by chess or bridge players. At other times, you are involved in performing an exacting, powerful physical skill. Physical precision often means the difference between a successful or unsuccessful round. If you get too "psyched up," you tend to lose precision and make inconsistent shots.

You have to play as though you have ice water in your veins. You can't let the excitement of the game or a given situation affect your play. Consistency dictates that you remain calm always. There is no place in golf for the emotionalism displayed by football or hockey players.

Part of keeping calm is not hitting the ball too hard. Too many beginning golfers, particularly men, try to hit the ball as though they're going for a home run at Yankee stadium. Try to hit the ball at about 80 percent of effort. Hit most of your shots exactly the same way, regardless of the club you are using. If you are on the fairway and feel you must really "crank" the ball with a 5-iron, drop to a 4- or 3-iron and take a relaxed swing. Taking a relaxed swing is an important part of keeping calm on the course.

Be Optimistic   Every golfer has had a beautiful drive land in the middle of a divot or hit a cart path and bounce into a water hazard. Don't worry about it. Say to yourself, "I got a bad break on that shot, but I will get plenty of good breaks in the future." Bad luck shots are part of the charm and unpredictability of the game. Don't dwell on the bad bounces and bad breaks because they have a way of evening themselves out. Think instead about the times you duffed the ball and had it land on the cart path and turn into a decent drive when it shouldn't have. Or, about the time you drove a ball into the rough only to hit a tree and have the ball bounce back onto the fairway. If you hit a bad shot or get a bad break, forget about it—think positively about the next shot. Erase the bad shots from your memory and look forward to the good shots to come.

Be Confident   Lack of confidence is a killer to the golfer. If you think you are going to hit a bad ball or come up short on a putt, you will. You have to approach every shot as though it is going to be perfect—forget about everything else. If you are hitting a ball close to a water hazard or bunker, forget about the hazard and concentrate on the target. As soon as you start thinking about where your ball *might* go if you make a mistake, your ball will almost invariably end up in the water. Think positively about every shot.

Concentrate!   Golf requires total concentration. If you are thinking about problems with your job or school, gridlock traffic on the way to the course, or a fight you had with your spouse, you will not play the game you are capable of playing. Work to block everything out of your mind during a shot except the task at hand. Don't be antisocial, but concentrate on every shot. Don't waste strokes by only going through the motions.

Arrive at the course early enough to warm up and get your mind on the game. This will help your concentration. The physical aspects of warm-up were discussed in Chapter 7. Warming up has psychological as well as physical benefits. Include in your warm-up routine time to visualize successful, well-executed shots. Use warm-up time to relax and help you iron out any last minute glitches in your game.

Don't Let Bad Shots or Bad Breaks Get You Down   This principle is an extension of "Be Optimistic." If you make a bad shot, forget about it and move onto the next. Everybody has bad shots and bad rounds. Often you will find that these are caused by a minor quirk that has developed in your swing, such as moving your head—something you can overcome with a lesson or additional practice. Even the pros fall back into bad habits they thought they had conquered. Bad shots and bad days are inevitable. Just as the stock market is subject to the ups and downs of the business cycle, so you are subject to the ups and downs of the golf cycle. Don't worry about it—it's part of the game.

Don't Try to Overcompensate for a Bad Shot   A common mistake of many golfers is to try to make up for a bad shot by hitting a spectacular winner on the next shot. Although taking a chance is sometimes worthwhile, going for "high risk, low percentage" shots every time you make a mistake is likely to cost you more strokes in the long run. In an impossible situation, it is sometimes better to hit the ball laterally or even backward so you have a clear shot at the green. You may give up a stroke, but you may be saving two or three strokes farther along.

In your mind, add one stroke to the hole when you make a big mistake. For example, you whiff at the ball and are one stroke down on a par 4; now play the hole as if it were a par 5. You may not get a spectacular score on the hole, but you are less likely to dig a hole for yourself by trying to overcompensate for your previous error.

Don't Try to Change Your Swing in the Middle of a Round
There is nothing more annoying than to have one of your well-meaning golf partners try to change your swing in the middle of a round. He or she may insist you change your grip, increase or decrease your turn, or change the position of your head. Don't try to make any changes until after the game. Otherwise, you will suffer from paralysis by analysis. You may get so confused by trying to change your technique that you find you can't do anything right.

Some people use "golf criticism" as a psychological tool to gain an advantage over opponents. They feel that if they can diminish your self-confidence, they will have an advantage. Don't let them do it. Ignore them and work on your game after the round is over.

On the golf course, concentrate only on the basics of the swing (grip, body position, stance, etc.). Recalling the fundamentals will make the greatest difference in how well you hit the ball. Be polite to critics, but don't attempt to make any changes until you are practicing with an instructor.

Play Every Shot to the Best of Your Ability   A round of golf takes a long time to play. As a consequence, it's easy to let your concentration lapse and find yourself merely going through the motions on some of your shots. Don't let it happen. Concentrate on every shot. Analyze every round so you get the most out of the game. If you practice this psychological principle consistently, you can take at least three to five strokes off your score every time you play.

Always Look for Opportunities to Save Strokes   Constantly analyze the course to look for advantages. If the situation warrants, you may find yourself, for example, going for the green from a fairway bunker or making a seemingly impossible shot from the trees. Weigh the situation and try the shot if you feel you have a reasonable chance for success. Looking for such opportunities will make the game more exciting and may lower your score.

Picture Successful Shots   *Mental imagery* is a psychological technique that has taken the sports world by storm. In this technique, golfers imagine that they are executing a perfect stroke before they actually hit the ball. This technique is based on the memory drum theory, according to which physical skills occur in a precise sequence that is imprinted on the brain.

Motor learning researchers (people who study how we learn physical skills such as the golf swing) have found that we perform sports skills in much the same way that a computer initiates a computer program. When you enter a command to begin a computer program, the computer retrieves information stored in its memory or on a disk and runs the program. When you begin a movement, a part of your brain called the cerebrum (the part of the brain involved in thought) and the motor cortex send signals to the spine and muscle fibers. Another part of the brain called the cerebellum constantly compares the intended with the actual movements and attempts to coordinate them. Mental imagery helps to ingrain a more precise movement pattern and helps some people perform better.

Before taking a shot, picture yourself performing the skill successfully. This may have two effects. First, it will increase your confidence level so you are more likely to make a successful shot. Second, it will reinforce correct motor patterns. Of course, it is critical that you visualize correct technique. If you visualize an incorrect swing, you are likely to reinforce bad habits.

Integrate your picturing a good swing with a feeling that you are going to make a good shot. However, don't think about it too long. If you do, you leave time for doubt and your mental rehearsal may backfire. Address the ball, take a few seconds to visualize a successful, well-executed shot, then do it—as President John Kennedy used to say—with vigor.

Don't Overanalyze Your Game   Stick with the basics and reduce the time you think about the nuances of the game. If you are hitting bad strokes, it is usually because of problems with fundamentals, such as moving your head or having an improper grip. Problems with the basics account for probably 99 percent of all the problems golfers have with their game.

Never Give Up   Sometimes unusual solutions to problems can save you strokes. For example, your ball lies to the right of a tree and you are a right-handed golfer. The tree is too big to reach around and effectively make a shot. Rather than declaring an unplayable lie or chipping the ball a few feet away, try hitting the ball left-handed using the toe of the club. This shot may be a bit awkward, but if you use a relatively fat club, such as a 4-iron, you may be able to hit a decent shot and save yourself a stroke. There are often novel ways around a problem. Rather than throwing a stroke away, try to think of an alternative.

Play the Percentages   Playing the percentages is an important psychological principle in golf. It means that you should make the shot that is least likely to get you into trouble. For example, if the straightest path between the hole and the ball is precariously close to being out of bounds, don't play the straightest path. Hit the ball to a fatter part of the fairway and play it from there so you don't risk a stroke and distance penalty. Also, sometimes you are better off risking going into the rough or bare ground than taking the chance of going into a water hazard and losing a stroke. You may actually have an easier shot to the green if the rough isn't too deep or the bare ground too hard.

Playing the percentages also means playing the hole according to your strengths, rather than according to what you would ideally like to do. Let's say you are playing a narrow fairway with deep rough and trees on either side. Rather than breaking out your driver, which may have been giving you nightmares lately, try playing a 3-wood, which you can control better. It might be very satisfying to get a big hit off the tee with your driver, but if you've been shanking these shots into the trees, don't do it. Play it safe and go for accuracy. Remember, the object of the game is to get the fewest strokes, not to hit the longest drive into the trees.

Or perhaps you slice the ball consistently. In this case, you may be better off playing the hole a little to the left of the pin, which will put you in excellent shape if the ball slices. Even if you hit the ball straight, your margin of error will not be excessive, and you will be in great shape for your next shot. If you hook the ball, though, you're in big trouble.

How do you know your strengths? If you play the same golf course regularly, make a map of your shots. Keep a small notebook in your bag, and use it to draw a picture of each hole and mark the location of each shot. You will see patterns emerge that will tell you a lot about your game. Not only will this technique help you better play the percentages based on your style of play, it will give you a clear picture of problems you are having with your game.

Try to play the shot that's easiest to hit. If you are playing a hole where the fairway is flat then abruptly goes downhill, it may be better to hit the ball shorter so your next shot is on level ground. If you hit the ball as far as you can, you may have to hit your next shot standing on the side of a hill, which is much more difficult. If you are on the apron of the green and the grass isn't too long, try using a putter rather than attempting to chip the ball on the green. As many golf pros have said, the best putt is usually better than the best chip. Play the percentages and you will lower your score.

Develop a Routine   Routines help you become more consistent. Try to develop a pattern of play you can carry from one round to the next. Arrive at the course in plenty of time to warm up. On the tee, check for wind direction. Observe what clubs opponents are using and how their shots have reacted on the course. On the green, consistently look for things such as green speed, the grain of the grass, breaks in the green. Look at these things systematically and don't overlook any of them.

When you practice, work on the skills that are going to make a difference. Usually, this means working on the basics. Work on one skill at a time. During one session you may work on body position, during another it may be weight shift. If you consistently work on the skills that make the most difference, you are more likely to become a low-scoring, consistent golfer.

Stress Quality When You Practice   Many golfers buy one or two large buckets of balls and hit them as though they were working out in a weight room. Golf is a game of precision. Make every practice shot count. Visualize every shot, as you do on the course. Give every practice shot a purpose. Play an imaginary game while on the practice tee. Shoot to a particular spot, rather than hitting the ball as far as you can.

Practice is a good time to learn how far you can typically hit a ball with each club. An irons chart says the average person hits a 9-iron 80 yards. Do you know how far you can hit one? Write down these distances and keep them in your bag.

Practice is the time to get correct motor patterns ingrained in your nervous system. You cannot do this if you are rushing your practice to hit 200 balls or if your technique has broken down because you're too tired. Take it slow and reflect on every shot.

Practice under realistic circumstances. Hitting from a mat or into a cage is different from hitting on a course. Try to find a practice range that lets you hit off an area that simulates a tee or fairway on a golf course. If you do, the skills you learn during practice will transfer easily to the golf course.

Play by the Rules   Playing by the rules sounds obvious, but it is amazing the number of players who disregard it. You can judge your progress and compare yourself with other golfers only if you play by the rules. If you take a Mulligan (an extra shot without penalty) every time you have a bad tee shot or kick the ball onto the fairway when you're in the rough, you might as well stay at the driving range. The rules are important in adding consistency to your game. You can judge your skill as a golfer and your improvement only if you play by a consistent set of rules. Carry a rule book in your bag. Rules and etiquette were discussed in Chapter 6.

Keep Up on the Latest Techniques   Be a student of your sport. Don't let the competition pass you by with improved playing techniques. Conversely, don't get sucked in by every fad that comes along. Read golf books and magazines, watch golf videos, talk to people about golf. After a while you'll be able to separate the worthwhile from the drivel.

Have Fun!   Having fun is probably the reason you play golf, so don't take the game too seriously. Golf is a wonderful game that allows you to go outdoors and be with friends. You get a chance to meet the challenge presented by great and breathtaking golf courses and to participate in an activity that pushes the mind and body. If you strive to make having fun your primary motivation for playing golf, you will be surprised how fast your game improves.

Worksheet

1. Name three mental elements of success in golf: _____,
_____, _____

2. The technique of picturing yourself making a perfect shot is called _____.

3. Name some basic psychological principles for becoming a better golfer._____

_____

_____

_____

_____

Glossary

Ace *See* a hole-in-one.

Address Occurs when you have taken your stance and grounded your club in preparation for hitting the ball. In a hazard, you have addressed the ball when you have taken your stance.

Ball in play A ball is in play after the player has made a stroke from the tee. It remains in play until it is sunk in the hole, is lost or out of bounds, or until another ball has been substituted (under the rules).

Birdie One stroke under par on a given hole.

Bogey One stroke over par on a given hole. Two strokes over par is called a double bogey.

Bunker A hazard—an area of bare ground usually covered by sand and often depressed.

Casual water Any temporary accumulation of water that's not a water hazard.

Cavity-back clubs Golf clubs that have weight taken out of the back of the club and concentrated on the sole, heel, and toe of the clubhead.

Championship tee The tee farthest from the hole and generally used in golf tournaments.

Chip A shot from near the green where most of the travel of the ball occurs on the ground.

Club lie The angle between the clubhead and the ground.

Course The area where play is permitted.

Distance A penalty requiring that you hit the ball from your original location (stroke and distance penalty).

Divot Hole made in the ground by a golf club.

Driver A metal or wooden-headed club used for hitting long shots from the tee. Usually designated as the #1 wood.

Driving range A place (usually a field) designated for practicing shots with your drivers and irons. Commercial driving ranges also usually have a putting green to practice putting.

Eagle   Two strokes under par for a given hole.

Fairway   The part of the golf course covered with short grass and extending from the teeing ground (tee) to the putting green.

Fat shot   A shot in which the player hits the ground behind the ball before making contact with the ball.

Flagstick   A cylindrical, movable straight indicator of the location of the hole.

Flex   The stiffness of the golf shaft.

Fore   The word you shout to warn players that you have hit a ball in their general direction and that they may be in danger of being hit.

Ground under repair   A designation made by the committee in charge of the course about a specific part of the course. In general (but not always), these areas are defined by stakes and lines drawn on the ground.

Handicap   Your rating as a golfer, which is established with the USGA. It is the average number of strokes you shoot above par.

Hazard   Any bunker, water hazard, or lateral water hazard.

Hitting the ball fat.   *See* fat shot.

Hole-in-one   Hitting the ball into the hole in one stroke from the teeing ground; an ace.

Honor   The side or person who is entitled to play first from the teeing ground. On the first tee, honor is decided by lot. After that, the person or side with the best score has the honor.

Hook   A shot in which the ball curves extremely right to left after it is hit.

Interlocking grip   A grip where the index finger of the top hand is interlocked with the little finger of the bottom hand.

Irons   golf clubs with metal, wedgelike club faces.

Irregular lies   A shot that requires you to address the ball in an abnormal stance (that is, on a slant, under a tree with a low overhanging branch, etc.).

Kiltie   A leather flap attached to the front of a golf shoe.

Lost ball   A ball not found or identified within minutes of searching for it. A ball is lost if another ball is put in play (under the rules) or a provisional ball is played from a position the original ball was likely to have been.

Match play   A scoring method where the winner is decided by the number of holes won.

Muscle-back clubs   Traditional golf clubs that have the weight concentrated in the center of the clubhead.

Obstruction   Anything artificial that is not considered an integral part of the course. Examples include movable benches, hoses, and rakes.

Opposing grip   A grip used in putting where the player grasps the club with palms facing each other.

Out of bounds   Ground on which play is prohibited.

Overlapping grip   A grip where the little finger of the right hand overlaps onto the forefinger of the left hand (reverse for left-handed players).

Par   The score an expert golfer would be expected to make for a given hole; it is based on the distance from the tee to the green.

Pitch   A short shot in golf, usually less than 100 yards, where the ball mainly travels in the air.

Pitching wedge   An iron with a very shallow club face used to make pitch shots.

Provisional ball   A ball played in case the ball in play is lost or is out of bounds.

Putter   A club to make putting shots from the green.

Putting green   A closely mowed grassy area that contains the hole and is specially prepared for putting.

Relief   The rule that allows players to move the ball and drop it elsewhere without penalty.

Reverse overlapping grip   A grip used in putting where the index finger of the top hand overlaps the ring finger of the right hand.

Rough   That part of the golf course left unmowed and uncultivated.

Sand Wedge   An iron with a very shallow club face and large flange on the bottom used to make shots from the sand.

Shank   A shot hit at a radical angle to its intended direction.

Slice   A shot in which the ball curves extremely left to right after it is hit.

Stance   Placing the feet in position to make a stroke.

Stroke   The forward movement of the club made with the intention of striking the ball. A voluntary checked swing is not a stroke. A player who swings and misses the ball has made a stroke.

Stroke play (medal play)   A scoring method where the winner is decided by the fewest number of strokes.

Tee box   *See* teeing ground.

Teeing ground   The starting place for the hole, it is the rectangular area (usually grass) two club lengths from back to front. Left and right boundaries (distance between these varies) are defined by tee markers.

Tee time   The time you are scheduled to begin your golf game.

10–finger grip   A grip where all ten fingers are in contact with the club. It is sometimes called the "baseball grip."

Topping   Hitting the top of the ball during a stroke.

USGA (United States Golf Association)   The governing body of golf in the United States. Together with the Royal and Ancient Golf Club of St. Andrews, the USGA is responsible for establishing the rules of golf.

Vardon grip   *See* overlapping grip.

Waggle   A small forward and backward movement of the club that's done before starting the swing.

Answers to Worksheets

Chapter 1

1. teeing ground
2. Play the ball where it lies.
3. Scotland, Holland
4. Royal and Ancient Golf Club of St. Andrews, United States Golf Association
5. executive courses

Chapter 2

1. golf clubs, bag, and balls
2. 14
3. shaft, club face
4. Long, short
5. grip, shaft, and club head
6. flexible (A), regular (R), and stiff (S)
7. Cavity-back
8. par
9. handicap
10. birdie
11. bogie

Chapter 3

1. fingers

2. Top hand: Rests in a line between the base of the little finger and the middle of the first segment of the index finger, thumb over the top of the club slightly turned to the right side of the handle

    Bottom hand: Grasps the club naturally, so that the club rests across the base of the first segment of the index finger and across the joint at the base of the little finger, the little finger of the bottom hand overlaps the left hand between the index and middle finger.

3. weight firmly and evenly distributed over both feet with the center of gravity running up the midline of the body, bend your knees and hips slightly, extend your arms naturally, right shoulder slightly below your left, arms and the club form and imaginary "y"

4. square

5. closed

6. back, open, together

7. open

8. parallel left

9. sternum or breastbone

10. head

11. trying to hit the ball too hard

12. slowly, smoothly

13. hands, arms, shoulders

14. proper weight shift, a good turning motion with the shoulders, a proper arc during your swing

15. pointing at the target

16. break them gradually and smoothly throughout the back swing, break them abruptly at the top of a swing

17. arc

18. hips

19. maintain the same arc

20. left

21. left, head

22. addressed

23. head, front, front

24. slice

25. hook

26. hit behind the ball

27. losing the extension of your arm during the swing

Chapter 4

1. opens, closer together, back slightly
2. on the side of potential trouble
3. the club head
4. flat portion of the bottom of the swing arc
5. further behind
6. Align yourself with the slope of the hill.
7. Strike the ball without hitting the ground in front of it.
8. ground the club
9. Contact the sand behind the ball.
10. mostly through the air
11. on the ground

Chapter 5

1. putts
2. overlapping, reverse overlap, and opposing
3. evenly between toes, heels, and left and right feet
4. Line up so your line of sight is over and slightly to the rear of the ball. Place the ball at or slightly to the rear of your left foot. Align the putter, your stance, and your line of sight either parallel or perpendicular to the hole.
5. pendulum
6. squarely
7. proportional to the distance of the putt
8. The movement of the ball will give you information about the slope and speed of the green.
9. 2

Chapter 6

1. Respect other players' concentration and well-being.
   Play briskly.
   Help maintain the course.
2. "fore"
3. Honor
4. Let other groups play through.
5. Don't take more than one practice swing.
   Replace all divots and repair ball-marks.
   Rake and smooth out bunkers after using them.
   Don't damage the greens.
   Don't litter.

6. match play, stroke play

7. provisional

8. one stroke and distance

9. obstruction

10. 2 strokes

11. 2 strokes

Chapter 7

1. Do endurance exercises that work major muscle groups, continuously, for a long period.
   Exercise above 50 percent of maximum capacity.
   Exercise for 15–60 minutes a session.
   Exercise 3–6 days a week.

2. endurance, strength, flexibility, and skill

3. increased muscle temperature, increased joint lubrication, increased circulation to exercising muscles, opportunity to practice

Chapter 8

1. belief, vision, and method

2. mental imagery

3. Find a good coach or golf instructor.
   Find people to play golf with.
   Keep calm.
   Be optimistic.
   Be confident.
   Concentrate.
   Don't let bad shots or bad breaks get you down.
   Don't try to overcompensate for a bad shot.
   Don't try to change your swing in the middle of a round.
   Play every shot to the best of your ability.
   Always look for opportunites to save strokes.
   Picture successful shots.
   Don't overanalyze your game.
   Never give up.
   Play the percentages.
   Develop a routine for playing a golf game or practice.
   Stress quality when you practice.
   Play by the rules.
   Keep up on the latest techniques.
   Have fun.

Index